Praise for
Stop Bush in 2004:
How Every Citizen Can Help

"This handbook for true activists is a must to help us save our democracy and Stop Bush from stealing another election. Simple, easy to do actions that carry a lot of power."

—Meria Heller, Webcaster and author of "The Awakening of an American."

"I can't recommend it enough!"

—Guy James, Liberal Talk Radio Host.

"Stop Bush in 2004" is pleasantly not about Bush bashing. Dobbins remains focused on emphasizing the importance of a campaigner being optimistic, informed and courteous, all of which he himself lives up to."

—Elizabeth Jamison Book Review in the Clemson University Tiger.

"For Every Joke there has been made about the damage Dubya has caused, Dobbins pens a page, a chapter, a mission in the hopes that maybe, just maybe, this time justice will prevail....What follows is a virtual how-to manual of governmental participation"

—*Bryan Jackson Book Review in the University of Arkansas at Little Rock Forum.*

Stop Bush In 2004

Stop Bush In 2004

◆

How Every Citizen Can Help

Second Edition

Michael John Dobbins

iUniverse, Inc.

New York Lincoln Shanghai

Stop Bush In 2004
How Every Citizen Can Help

iUniverse, Inc.

For information address:
iUniverse, Inc.
2021 Pine Lake Road, Suite 100
Lincoln, NE 68512
www.iuniverse.com

ISBN: 0-595-31644-1

Printed in the United States of America

For Humanity

"The World is my country,
all mankind are my brothers,
and my religion is to do good"

—Thomas Paine, author of "Common Sense"
And a Founding Father of the United States
of America

Contents

Acknowledgments

Without the aid of numerous individuals this book would not be the book it is today. Moreover, it may have never been written. Whether you agree with this book or not, I'm going to thank you.

Ayako, you are my teacher and my encouragement. Thank you for your true friendship and for making my life more colorful than I ever thought possible.

I thank my family for their love, support, and extremely good advice, especially my mother and father. Also Kelly, Sarah, and Grandpa John. Thank you for being there if and when I need you. Uncle Mike, Aunt Ginny, Grandma and Grandpa Dobbins, Aunt Mary, Uncle Ron, Cousin Mary, Ron, Kitty, Erin, Carrie, and everyone else.

The town of Naperville and all my friends back home including Alex, Steve, Mike M., Mike C. Mike H., Shaun, Jason, Chris, Josh, Brian, Dan, Bridget, Sarah, Doris, Carolyn, Stephanie, Kim, Liz, Reina, Anna, Eileen, Chris C., Shephali, Steve Z., Sonya G., Robin, Gen, Rob E., Cheryl M., Scott and Kristy V., The Beytien Family, everyone at Patterson Elementary, everyone at Little Friends, My teachers: Mr Eby, Mrs. D, Mr. Jeske, Mr Shneider, Mr. Ley, Mr. Merek, Mr. Maxstadt, Mr. Wall, Mrs. Prattel, Mr. Monahan, Mr. Young, Mrs. Dumphey, Mrs. Dice, Mrs. K. Ms. Otto, Mrs. Cushing, Mrs, Johnson, Mrs. Erant, Mrs. Dolenberg, Mrs. Tredwell, and anyone I may have missed.

Albion College and the town of Albion, Michigan. Especially Andy K., Michelle K., Joe S., Katie S., Valerie M., Kierston, Kevin K., Jen B., Abby, Andrew S., Rob S., Paul K., Jon E., Maria A, Zulehka H., Warwick, Morisolo. Professors and Administration I'd like to thank include Coach Egnatuk, Dr. Dick, Dr. Brumfiel, Dr. Hooks, Dr. Perusek, Dr. Wilson, Dr. Bollman, Dr. Anderson, Dr. Fryxell, Dr. Raj, Vera W., President Mitchell, Warren and Mr. C, and all the others I may have missed.

Everyone at the bank, thank you for your friendships. Jen, Joe, Joe L., Rick, Brian, Ron, Sally, Kristin, Heidi, Cheryl, Jon, Laura, Anthony, and Al.

Nature's Classroom and the east coast have been very kind to me. I thank all who have taught and inspired me. Jean, Mary S., Sarah, Richard, Joe Don, Madeline, Liz, Anka, Matt G., Matt O., KT, Stephan, J. Santos, Lela, Chris, Kerrie, Eddie, Dee, Gil, Rebecca, Deforest, Heather, Adrian, Patrick, Mary B., Lindsay, Jason, Leo, Joey, Clara, Amy, Chris L., Marc, October, Carolyn, Kate S., Raph, Jessica, Annie, Tim, Dave D., Stew, Kip, Desmond, Scott, Emma, Sophie, Jenny, Sarah, Antero, Xavier, Luke, Adam, Andrew, Tomcat, Jones, Maureen, and everyone else who I may have missed.

Clark University and the city of Worcester, Massachusetts were essential to completing this book quickly and efficiently. Thank you especially to Irena, Jenne, and Ayako, my flat mates. Stella, Scott, Lou, Sarah, everyone at the Public Library, and Clark's library.

Lastly, without music and books to inspire me, I don't know where I would have found the motivation for this book. Thank you to Pearl Jam, Radiohead, Rage Against The Machine, R.E.M., and Beethoven for putting out such great music. Also works by Kurt Vonnegut, Daniel Quinn, Howard Zinn, Noam Chomsky, Jean Liedloff, and Ayn Rand.

Round 2

Since the books publication I have received the support of numerous individuals, without whom the book and the "Stop Bush" message would not have been as successful. I will do my best to thank everyone.

In the realm of radio I would like to thank Meria Heller, Steve Kass and Jeff Wade, Charlie and Ernie, Jordan Levy, Mike Turner, Guy James and Gene, Mike Webb, Louie Free, Doug Basham, John McMullen and Charlie Dyer, Jamie Allman and Max Foizey, Dori Smith, Jeremy Cordeaux and Jacqui Munn.

Websites include www.DemocraticUnderground.com, www.Buzzflash.com, www.Democrats.us, www.DemsOnline.net, www.Democrats.com, www.Go-Left.org, www.MichaelMoore.com, www.JimPillsbury.org, the Politizine blog spot, and countless others who have linked up to my website.

Additionally, I'd like to thank the new people I've had a chance to meet as a result of the book and website. Barbra Bell and Alan Frankel: Thanks for your book suggestions and advice. Also Nellie Wolf, Valerie Hass, Herb Chasem, Megan Przygoda, Eric Freud, R.J., Amy Mosher, David Coyne, Maureen Schwab, Jack, Mary, Art, Adam Freudberg, Jason Pollens, Lynne, Dori Smith, Leigh Novog, Kelly Momberger, Liz Kotowski, Seema Tewari, and Kate Casa.

Moreover I'd like to thank Howard Dean, John Kerry, John Edwards, Al Franken, Joe Conason, Jim Hightower, Norman Solomon, and Michael Moore.

Many organizations and publications have helped along the way. Thank you to Tatnuck Booksellers (Sarah, Beth, Tom, and Matt), Harvard Bookstore (Molly), WordsWorth Bookstore (Martha), In City Times (Rose), Worcester

Telegram and Gazette (Richard and Shaun), Worcester Magazine, The Boston Phoenix (Camille and Susan), The Metro West (Sarah), The University of Arkansas at Little Rock Forum (Bryan), The Clemson University Tiger (Elizabeth), The Brattleboro Reformer, The Progressive Democrats of Massachusetts, Clark University Democrats, Worcester Public Library, Ward 8, The Nation, In These Times, The Progressive, ZMag, PRweb, and Planned Parenthood.

Preface

With the Presidential Election slowly creeping up on us, American's disillusioned by President Bush may be asking themselves "What can I do to stop Bush from being elected?" Well, I hope to get you started.

See, I asked the same question back in April of 2003; when the war with Iraq was supposedly "won" and "over". After deep contemplation and thought, the answer came to me: Write a book! Write a book for the millions of disenchanted Americans who see Bush and his administration for what they really are. Give them concrete methods of action to affect voters and remove Bush from office. Thus, the decision regarding what I would do to defeat the President was made.

I began conducting extensive research in regards to political and social activism, political campaigns, Bush's record as President, politics, and the current political scene. June and July would prove to be the most focused months of my entire life.

10 re-writes, 8 gallons of orange juice, and hundreds of hours at the library later the book was complete: *Stop Bush in 2004: How Every Citizen Can Help*. Since August of 2003, my full time job has been telling the world about it.

To date, I have mailed out over 200 copies of the book, conducted 11 radio interviews, appeared in numerous newspaper articles, given speeches, handed out pamphlets, written articles, and talked with hundreds of voters.

Apparently, all of my hard work is beginning to pay off. "Stop Bush in 2004" has sold enough copies and garnered enough attention that it was time to make a 2nd edition.

Stop Bush in 2004 is a comprehensive action handbook for every American with the desire to defeat George W. Bush in 2004. Within its pages are effective ways of taking action to influence the Bush Campaign, the Democratic Campaign, improve media coverage, engage students, and affect the economy. In addition, I have provided educational and organizational materials, a brief history of Bush's record, a campaign calendar, and an abundance of resources. Every section has been updated and expanded with additional information and resources. *Stop Bush in 2004* will provide support for all taking action to defeat President Bush.

Only with millions of Americans taking action does the Bush juggernaut have a chance at being defeated. For this reason, I urge every American to get involved and take action against Bush and after the election, to stay involved in politics.

If there is one thing I've learned since starting this journey, it is this: We are not asking enough of our citizens. Vote? This is not enough. Write a letter? Send an e-mail? These are not enough. We must get involved in politics on a regular basis, with regular participation and action. Not just a few more individuals; everyone. We must work to change our culture and our personal lifestyles so all Americans participate in politics at the local, state, and national level. Participating in politics can become as popular and as expected as watching television, but each of us must work to change ourselves and those around us if it is to occur.

Only when we are empowered as individual citizens can we empower those who represent us to do the right thing. So, challenge yourself, build your confidence, and empower those around you. Then we will achieve the big changes we long for.

I'm asking you and all Americans to make a commitment starting with the 2004 Presidential Campaign to do *more* than vote. **Get empowered and get involved!**

Michael John Dobbins

1

Introduction

On November 7, 2000, I proudly strode into the voting both and cast my ballot for the Presidential candidate I thought was best. I voted for the candidate who, I believed, was the most honest, principled, and had the better vision for our country. I voted for Ralph Nader. Not only did I vote for Nader, I also volunteered for the Nader Campaign. I passed out literature, put up signs, donated money, and encouraged others to vote for him.

Why? Because I was fed up with the two major political parties. I was fed up with the taking of preposterous amounts of money from corporations. I was fed up with them acting as though they weren't influenced by corporate contributions. The only interests I saw being served were those of the wealthy, not those of the average people. The differences between Republicans and Democrats seemed inconsequential at the time. To me, the most urgent problems were getting corporate money out of politics and making sure the Green Party received 5 percent of the vote to qualify for federal campaign funds.

For what it's worth, I know now that I didn't fully comprehend the consequences of supporting a third party. Moreover, I didn't fully realize the very important differences between the major parties. I along with millions of other Nader voters have learned my lesson. Mr. Nader, it appears, has not.

I understood that voting for a third party might help get George W. Bush elected, but I did not grasp the consequences of having a Bush administration in office. I was not alone. Various news reports and opinion polls have since confirmed my suspicion that millions of Americans did not foresee how dangerous a Bush administration would be.

If I had known then what I know now, I like to think I would have wised up and voted for Al Gore. Now that I fully understand the consequences of a Bush presidency, a Republican presidency, I am prepared to support John Kerry or whoever else may receive the nomination. There *are* differences between Democrats and Republicans, despite what anyone, including Ralph Nader, might say.

With that understanding, my priorities have changed. Although I still disagree with the two party system and hate the thought of corporations buying our politicians and policy makers, I realize that the most pressing problem facing America today is the presidency of George W. Bush.

President Bush is trampling our civil liberties by threatening our rights of free speech, privacy, choice, and due process. President Bush has squandered the financial future of our nation with huge tax cuts for the rich that have created record deficits. President Bush has turned the Oval Office into a corporate boardroom in which his campaign contributors create legislation. President Bush imposed his religious beliefs on national policy. President Bush has misled America into a war that has nothing to do with terrorism. That war to date has cost 551 American soldiers their lives, it has cost taxpayers hundreds of billions of dollars, and there is no end in sight. President Bush has inflated the military budget to over $400 Billion a year but cut funds for domestic programs. President Bush, through his actions, has served the interests of the haves and ignored the needs of the have-nots.

President Bush's actions have opened my eyes to what's good about the Democratic Party and why it's so important to support it. I have come to the conclusion that the Democrats, despite their flaws, have a world view that is close to my own and will be better for the majority of Americans. I support the Democrats because they are established, they share many of my values, and because they give me a voice. When they promote policies with which I agree I will tell them of my support. When they do something with which I disagree as they are bound to do, I will speak up loudly and make my opposition known. This is what political power is if you are a citizen. By supporting the Democrats, I at least have the chance to influence policy and affect how they vote. If I support a third party, I have no representation and no influence.

An important aspect of the election to remember is that voting for the Democrats and removing Bush from office does not only mean the removal of Bush, it means Bush and his *entire* administration are gone. A vote for the Democrat is also a vote against Cheney, Ashcroft, Rumsfeld, Ridge, Powel, Norton, Rove, Rice, Card, Wolfowitz, Abraham, and all the other players. Luckily for us, the election is right around the corner.

As important as ending George W. Bush's presidency is, there is much more at stake in the 2004 election. In June of 2003, I heard a speech by David Gergen, the columnist and commentator who was an advisor to the Nixon, Ford, Reagan, and Clinton administrations. He made perfectly clear that Karl Rove and the Republicans are hoping to establish Republican dynasty. They seek to take control of Congress, The Judiciary, and the White House not only in 2004, but also in 2006, 2008, 2010, 2012 and beyond. To not have a 51-49 majority in the Senate, but a 60-40 majority. To not have four or five conservative Supreme Court Justices, but seven or eight. The Republicans are working to control the federal government long into the future. If the thought of four more years of George W. Bush makes you uneasy, how do you feel about an additional eight years of his brother Jeb? And remember, there would be Republican majorities in the House, Senate, and Supreme Court. November 2, 2004 is our chance to set back the Republican machine and write our own history.

As I write this in March of 2004, Bush has begun to sink in the polls. I only hope this is the beginning of a mass awakening of Americans to Bush's deceptions and harmful policies. While the Bush administration first gave the impression that they would easily triumph in November, there is much they are beginning to worry about and a great deal they secretly fear. They are haunted by George H. Bush's 1992 defeat to Bill Clinton. They know how easily the nation's approval, and along with it the election, can be lost. Moreover, a number of problems are lurking in the political shadows, any one of which could bring the administration down:

1. *The economy.* It feels like it's been in the blender ever since Bush took office. If it continues to worsen, Bush will have a difficult time convincing Americans he deserves four more years.

2. *The collapse of Iraq.* It's already unstable and could disintegrate at any moment. Total chaos, civil war, mass civil disobedience, or a public uprising all possibilities. This would shatter the little trust that is left in Bush's foreign policy abilities.

3. *God forbid, another terrorist attack.* If a terrorist attack to the likes of Sept. 11th occurs, questions as to whether or not Bush is up to the job for this war on terror will be raised. The new terrorist attack will be fresh in people's minds and their confidence in Bush will wane.

4. *Investigations and revelations.* The corporate media giants are starting to actually do their job and ask whether the Bush administration mislead or lied to the American people regarding the weapons of mass destruction Iraq supposedly possessed. Additionally, there is the 9/11 investigation which Bush has done his best to disrupt, and the investigation into who in the Whitehouse

leaked a covert CIA agents name. Depending on the outcomes of the investigations, Bush's campaign could be greatly set back.

5. *Door Number Five.* What's behind door number five? If only the Bush team knew. This is the unknown; the unpredictable. Things the Bush administration cannot control, address, or contemplate. Perhaps a reporter breaking an important story, Bush performing horrible in a debate, or the people of America realizing John Kerry and the Democratic Party are much better suited to serve their interests. Or, perhaps it is something else entirely, something like this book...

The purpose of this book is to encourage, motivate, and educate citizens to take action during the 2004 presidential campaign to stop Bush from being elected. America deserves a much better President, leader, and administration; but deserving and getting are two different things. We must participate, not only in this election, but here on out, on every political level possible. We as citizens must take responsibility for our government and the decisions it makes in our name.

Although tens of millions of people across America are disillusioned with the Bush administration; most do little or nothing about it. I know. I used to be one of them. I've always paid attention to political matters but I rarely participated. It took watching the Bush administration implement its vision of the world to get me involved. Those who aren't politically active are caught in a vicious circle; they don't participate because they feel the government doesn't do anything for them, and the government doesn't do anything for them because they don't participate. The only way out is to get involved. By choosing to participate, you have the possibility of being heard, shaping policy, and realizing your vision of the world.

Yes, your vision of the world. We cannot simply oppose Bush for the sake of opposing him. I oppose Bush because his vision of the world is completely at odds with mine. In my vision, the president recognizes a woman's right to control her body, respects and conserves the natural environment, and provides the public with pride and confidence rather than fear and conformity. In my vision of the world, the President promotes human rights, worker's rights, and children's rights; a fair trade system that prioritizes rights over profit; a foreign policy that recognizes every human's right to exist, works for peace, and does not act above the law. A different vision of the world is why I'm so strongly opposed to George W. Bush. Whatever your world vision might be, it is up to you to work and make it a reality.

It is our collective responsibility to participate in government using whatever means of participation best suits our own personal style, beliefs, and strengths. In the following pages, I describe numerous ways to take action, educate yourself, and organize. Read the entire book and select those actions that are best for you.

For additional resources, actions, and updates throughout the presidential campaign, please visit the website <u>www.StopBushin2004.com</u>

2

Education

As an educator, I am predisposed to emphasize the importance of this section. Education is the most fundamental of actions a citizen can take. One cannot take action or much less consider taking action if they aren't informed on what it is they need to know. If you're reading this book then you are most likely already educated on why George W. Bush's policies are awful for our country.

Although millions of Americans are aware of the danger Bush poses, they are missing an important quality which you have learned; the knowledge that you can change things. Often times when I discuss with people why they don't take action I usually receive a response to the effect that "the system" is too corrupted, the problems are too big for them to make a difference, or that however much they care and want to change things; they simply don't have the time or energy. You on the other hand have gone over this landfill of the mind, taken out the trash, and in the garbage's place discovered a garden full of possibilities. I commend you and hope you will take the next steps, continuing your education and taking action.

This chapter will provide you with what and how you should educate yourself with now, during the campaign, and there after. There is much to know and the political climate is constantly changing. Many people assume they already know everything, or they know what they know is correct, or that they don't need to know, all of which are dangerous for anyone going to take action. I urge everyone to educate themselves prior to taking action, while you're taking action, and once the campaign is over. For those who may doubt the need for education, please reconsider. I emphasize this not only because I'm an educator, but because I want a Democratic president and administration. The more educated people are when taking their actions, the better chance we have. Consider the following advantages:

- An educated person is more confident in themselves when communicating with others.

- Your knowledge gives you a professional appearance which enables others to take you seriously.

- Education gives you the tools to be more persuasive when communicating and the know how to communicate to a particular audience.

- The knowledge gained makes one more effective when taking action and a better citizen.

The bottom line; the more you know the better for you and the country.

Now that I hoped to have convinced you to take your education seriously, you must know where, how, and what to educate yourself in. (I've already given you the why, and the when is obvious, now!)

WHERE: The Internet, public library, books, magazines, newspapers, local bookstores, and college library's are all wonderful places to find resources.

HOW: Watch, listen, and read about the subjects you need to know. As you do, be a critical thinker. Separate opinions from facts and question the content and the source. Why is the individual making this slant in the story? What are they not saying? What is their motive for saying this? Also, seek out professionals for their advice.

WHAT: Before you can do anything, you must know *what* you need to know. The Electoral College, making your vote count, campaign issues and records, the current political scene, activist image, and your action of choice should all be well known. Here is a brief overview of the six.

ELECTORAL COLLEGE

The purpose of every action contained in this book is to affect how people will vote. In whatever action you take, you must keep in mind the Electoral College, for this is how Presidents are elected. For those who were in the dark during the 2000 election, Al Gore received the popular vote and did not obtain the presidency. Our system is not based on who obtains the most votes. Our system is based on each state being worth a set number of electoral votes, the candidate with the popular vote in each state wins that states electoral votes, and which ever candidate gets to the magic number of 270 electoral votes, even if he breaks the law in the process, becomes president. Thus, every single vote for the loser in a state does not count. This is an important lesson to remember. Rather than focusing our efforts on simply obtaining more votes, we must strategize to affect the voters in a *particular state* because it is the Electoral College that matters, not how many votes each candidate receives. We can help the Democrat win the presidency by focusing our actions according to which states the Democrat can win.

For example, although I don't want to concede any state to Bush, it is likely that he will win his home state of Texas. Thus, the truth of the matter is, if you're a Democrat in Texas and vote in Texas, the only votes that count are state and local. Your presidential vote doesn't mean a thing. You may be asking yourself "What in blazes can I do about it!?!" Well, if you're a Democrat in Texas, rather than focus all your efforts on Texas, focus some efforts on a neighboring state where the Democrat has a good chance at winning. (Louisiana, New Mexico, and Arkansas) I'm not advocating to move there (but feel free to if you'd like), but neighboring states that have a fighting chance are worth taking action in. On the flip side, if you reside in Massachusetts or Vermont, both of which should easily go to the Democrat, focus instead on New Hampshire, Maine, and Pennsylvania. Always keep in mind this is a state by state fight.

The following are statistics to consider from the 2000 Presidential election campaign. It provides the states initials, how many electoral votes the state is worth (updated for 2004), the percentage of eligible voters that turned out, and who won the state in 2000. The statistics are from the book "The Perfect Tie", by James W. Ceaser and Andrew Busch. There is a full bibliography at the back of the book for your convenience. The last column (2004) is one that I have provided to give you an idea of which states are likely (L) to vote Bush (L-BUSH), Democrat (L-DEM), or Either.

STATE	Electoral Votes	Turnout	2000	2004
Alabama	9	50%	BUSH	L-BUSH
Alaska	3	66%	BUSH	L-BUSH
Arizona	10	42%	BUSH	**EITHER**
Arkansas	6	48%	BUSH	**EITHER**
California	55	44%	GORE	L-DEM
Colorado	9	57%	BUSH	**EITHER**
Connecticut	7	58%	GORE	L-DEM

STATE	Electoral Votes	Turnout	2000	2004
Delaware	3	56%	GORE	L-DEM
Florida	27	51%	BUSH	**EITHER**
Georgia	15	44%	BUSH	**EITHER**
Hawaii	4	40%	GORE	L-DEM
Idaho	4	54%	BUSH	L-BUSH
Illinois	21	53%	GORE	L-DEM
Indiana	11	49%	BUSH	**EITHER**
Iowa	7	61%	GORE	**EITHER**
Kansas	6	54%	BUSH	L-BUSH
Kentucky	8	52%	BUSH	L-Bush
Louisiana	9	54%	BUSH	**EITHER**
Maine	4	67%	GORE	**EITHER**
Maryland	10	52%	GORE	L-DEM
Massachusetts	12	57%	GORE	L-DEM
Michigan	17	58%	GORE	**EITHER**
Minnesota	10	69%	GORE	**EITHER**
Mississippi	6	49%	BUSH	L-Bush
Missouri	11	58%	BUSH	**EITHER**
Montana	3	62%	BUSH	L-BUSH
Nebraska	5	56%	BUSH	L-BUSH
Nevada	5	44%	BUSH	**EITHER**
New Hamp.	4	62%	BUSH	**EITHER**
New Jersey	15	51%	GORE	L-DEM
New Mexico	5	47%	GORE	**EITHER**
New York	31	49%	GORE	L-DEM
N. Carolina	15	50%	BUSH	L-BUSH
North Dakota	3	60%	BUSH	L-BUSH

STATE	Electoral Votes	Turnout	2000	2004
Ohio	20	60%	BUSH	**EITHER**
Oklahoma	7	49%	BUSH	L-BUSH
Oregon	7	61%	GORE	**EITHER**
Pennsylvania	21	54%	GORE	**EITHER**
Rhode Island	4	54%	GORE	L-DEM
S. Carolina	8	46%	BUSH	L-BUSH
South Dakota	3	58%	BUSH	L-BUSH
Tennessee	11	49%	BUSH	**EITHER**
Texas	34	43%	BUSH	L-BUSH
Utah	5	53%	BUSH	L-BUSH
Vermont	3	64%	GORE	L-DEM
Virginia	13	52%	BUSH	L-BUSH
Washington	11	57%	GORE	**EITHER**
West Virginia	5	46%	BUSH	**EITHER**
Wisconsin	10	66%	GORE	**EITHER**
Wyoming	3	60%	BUSH	L-BUSH
DC	3	49%	DEM	L-DEM

Please remember that the 2004 projections are just that, projections, and in reality anything is possible. The Bush campaign has publicly stated they are going to make a serious effort to contend in the 2000 Democratic won states of Pennsylvania, New York, Connecticut, New Jersey, New Mexico, Oregon, Minnesota, California, and Wisconsin. The choice of what actions to take in what state are on an individual level. Do what you think is best by taking the time to consider what swing state(s) you will take action in. Remember, it's not about just getting more votes. It's about getting more votes in particular states. Here is a list of which states are up for grabs, potentially up for grabs, and unlikely up for grabs.

Swing States: Florida, Iowa, Maine, Michigan, Minnesota, Missouri, Nevada, New Hampshire, New Mexico, Ohio, Oregon, Pennsylvania, Tennessee, Washington, West Virginia, and Wisconsin.
Potential Swing States: Arizona, Arkansas, California, Colorado, Georgia, Indiana, Louisiana, and Virginia.
Republican States: Alabama, Alaska, Idaho, Kansas, Kentucky, Mississippi, Montana, Nebraska, North Carolina, North Dakota, Oklahoma, South Carolina, South Dakota, Texas, Utah, and Wyoming.
Democrat States: Connecticut, Delaware, D.C., Hawaii, Illinois, Maryland, Massachusetts, New Jersey, New York, Rhode Island, and Vermont.

Make Your Vote Count:

From the ashes of the 2000 Florida recount disaster came the Help America Vote Act (HAVA) passed by Congress in the fall of 2002. HAVA compels states to upgrade their voting machines prior to the 2004 election. While the intentions of HAVA may have been good, reality suggests another election disaster. If you think your vote will count in 2004, think again.

The electronic voting machines states are scrambling to purchase have been proven to contain numerous flaws. According to www.VerifiedVoting.org, secret software within the computer to track votes has been approved by courts; all software and hardware has the potential for bugs; secret programs could be installed without detection; hackers can tamper with the machines; and some software allows you to cast an unrestricted amount of votes! Electronic democracy? Not even close.

Now you might be thinking to yourself, "Wait a minute. Isn't there a paper record we can check when discrepancies occur?" Well, not any more. HAVA meant to require a paper record, but the new law is being "interpreted" by many to mean: only when an audit is necessary. Of course, this would result in the computer dispensing the exact results it already had in its system. The computer will never be wrong! The public will never know if the computer recorded their vote correctly, and no physical evidence will be available to prove otherwise.

Flawed computers, no paper record—you'd think it couldn't get any worse, right? Here's the kicker; Walden O'Dell, CEO of Diebold, a major supplier of voting machines, is a staunch supporter of President Bush. In a fund-raising letter in 2003 O'Dell had the nerve to state that he was "committed to helping Ohio deliver its electoral votes to the president next year."

Fortunately, David Dill has created **www.VerifiedVoting.org** to draw attention to the problem and encourage citizen support for proposed solutions. Representative Rush Holt (D-N.J.) has introduced HR 2239 and Senator Bob Graham (D-FL) has created S.1980 to protect American voters.

The Voter Confidence and Increased Accessibility Act of 2003 calls for all states to create a paper record of votes prior to casting votes on a machine. Thus, if there were any questions regarding the accuracy of the machines, real paper ballots would be available as the vote of final record.

Every reader can do something about this now: Visit www.VerifiedVoting.org and sign the petition; call your state, local and federal representatives; contact your secretary of state, and tell others. We need to make a big deal out of this because it is a big deal, and it's not getting the attention it deserves. Democracy and the right to vote should be taken seriously whenever threatened. Both remain at stake in 2004, four years after the last electoral debacle. If you haven't yet, please visit www.VerifiedVoting.org and www.BlackBoxVoting.com today.

CAMPAIGN ISSUES AND RECORDS

Currently the major issues of the 2004 campaign are shaping up to be: jobs, the war in Iraq, the war on terror, health care, the budget deficit, social security, homeland security, the environment, corporate corruption (hopefully), and the Supreme Court. It is essential to know where Bush and his administration stand on these issues, what his record of 4 years proves, and where the Democratic candidate stands. Knowledge, as they say, is power. When the Democratic candidate is selected, the issues will start to take shape and the differences between the two candidates should be crystal clear. At a minimum, know the key issues of the campaign and where each candidate stands. As always, the more you know, the more effective you'll be at taking action.

The last chapter of this book provides a brief overview of Bush's record. In addition, a list of Democratic contact information is located in the back. Please utilize these resources during the campaign.

Websites:

www.Democrats.org/Specialreports
www.Thousandreasons.org
www.truthaboutgeorge.com
www.BushWatch.net

www.TheNation.com
www.InTheseTimes.com
www.Buzzflash.com

Books:

Bushwacked by Molly Ivans and Lou Dubose
The Bush Haters Handbook by Jack Huberman
The Great Unraveling by Paul Krugman
The Lies of George W. Bush by David Corn
You Back the Attack, We'll Bomb Who We Want! with commentary by the Center for Constitutional Rights and remixed war propaganda by Micah Ian Wright.

CURRENT POLITICAL SCENE

Keeping up on the latest in the political world, especially during an election year, is a must. Things change in the blink of an eye. Keep yourself in tune to how both parties are running their campaigns, what the media covers, and what the public is saying. If a major story breaks, analyze how to use it to your advantage in your chosen action. You are trying to affect the political scene so it is crucial to stay updated. This goes not only for the national picture, but your local and state political scene as well. Your state or city may represent the candidates and the campaign in a completely different light then that of the national media. Here is what you should do to stay up to date:

POLITICAL PARTIES: Read the liberal and conservative magazines. Most if not all of them can be found at your local bookstore, Borders, and Barnes and Noble. Additionally most of the magazines post their content online. For the Democrats read The Nation, The New Republic, The American Prospect, In These Times, and The Progressive. The websites of www.Buzzflash.com, www.Democrats.us, and the daily E-mail newsletter from www.CenterforAmericanProgress.org and www.Democrats.com are essential. For Bush and his administration read The National Review, The Weekly Standard, The American Spectator, or The American Conservative.

OVERALL PICTURE: Giant media corporations, who don't have our best interest in mind, will shape the overall picture of the campaign and the candidates. Nonetheless, most Americans get their news from them so we must pay attention to what they say. For the big picture read the corporate controlled mass media such as the Washington Post, New York Times, or L.A. Times and major weekly magazines such as Time or Newsweek. Watch one of the major national nightly newscasts (they're all the same anyway) and your local news to learn what they're reporting about the campaigns. If you so dare, watch some of the cable "news" shows, National Public Radio and C-Span T.V.

Activist Image:

Much of the following is probably common sense, but since our passion to defeat Bush is so great and millions of citizens will be taking action for the first time, it must be discussed.

Whenever we take action, we must keep in mind our public image. How we act, speak, and look all represent the Democratic Campaign. Whenever we are interacting with voters they see more than the issues, they see an extension of the Democratic nominee himself. We represent the Democrats and the Democratic nominee in every action we take. As a result, we must make sure every word that comes out of our mouth, every change in our body language, and every piece of clothing we wear reflects the image we want to project. A few things to consider:

Attitude: Positive, confident, outgoing, patient, open to questions and complaints.

Clothing and Accessories: Presentable, nothing offensive, nothing too radical.

Language and Body Language: Non-offensive, non-aggressive, respectful, always honest, not afraid to say "I don't know", as if you were talking with your grandparents.

Like I said, most of this is common sense, but its importance must not be underestimated. If we want to persuade average Americans that we're right, then we must think like them. This means no pins comparing Bush to Hitler, no arguments (even if they try to start one), no insults if they support Bush, and no sighing if they still want to think about it. We must do everything in our power to present ourselves in a good light and leave voters with a positive impression of us and the Democrats.

ACTION OF CHOICE

Choosing the method of action you will take is an individual choice. As you read this book, be conscious of which actions you're drawn towards. Being passionate about your choice will make you a better activist. Working in a way you're not enjoying or truly believing in is not healthy for you or the cause you're addressing. The more confident you are, the more you'll enjoy the action you take and the more effective you'll be. Unfortunately you cannot take every action mentioned within the book. Find a few you are passionate about and educate yourself to the full extent on that method of action. While I describe many of the actions you can take, there is always more you can learn.

Once you've read the book and know what type of action(s) you yearn to take, start as soon as possible (but don't forget to educate yourself). On the other hand, after reading this book you discover you're not confident in what action to take, ask yourself these questions:

What campaign issue motivates me the most?
What talents do I have to offer to a particular type of action?
What action can I picture myself taking?
What actions am I comfortable or uncomfortable with?
What action do I feel will have the most effect on getting more votes for the Democrat?

You can then base your actions on which answers are most important to you.

If, however, you're still struggling, talk with friends and family members. After all, they know you best. Whichever type of person you are, the most urgent matter after reading this book is to take action. Our country needs more of its citizens participating now more than ever.

Further Reading: "Politics for Dummies" by Ann DeLaney
           "Enough is Enough: The Hellraiser's Guide to
           Community Activism" by Diane MacEachern.

3

Organizing

I come across many people who are reluctant to organize their own group or for that matter even participate with an organization already in place. I've heard reasons ranging from they don't know the people well enough, don't agree with the organization 100%, or they are simply lazy. This attitude is not only dangerous, but goes entirely against the ideals of our country; brotherhood, charity, and equality. We would not have the freedoms we have today if it were not for people who put their own self-interest aside and saw the bigger picture, the common goal which all of them had. Furthermore, we may not have our freedoms of tomorrow if we do not come together in a similar fashion. If individuals maintain a position of unwilling to compromise, then we can expect four more years of Bush, Cheney, Rumsfeld, and the rest of the gang. Keep focused on the common goal we all have; removing Bush from office. That's what matters, and that's how we'll succeed. Some of the benefits of organizing include:

- Meeting new and interesting people who share the same passions as you.
- Through the organizing process you are improving your own skills at putting things in order.
- You have the chance to educate people on your ideas and can hear new ones.

Organizing before you take action will vastly increase the probability that your action will be successful. That is why we're taking action in the first place, right? No one is playing to lose, so we must do everything necessary to increase our chances of winning. Here are some steps in organizing.

Groups Already Formed:

My hunch is that most people will want to join a local group that is already formed. Nearly every community should have a local group working on behalf of the Democratic candidate. I highly suggest joining them, even if you aren't fond of the Democratic Party or nominee. We all agree on one thing: George W. Bush must be defeated and the Democrat is the only candidate who stands a chance. Please check out the "Democratic Contacts" or visit the websites: www.Democrats.org, www.MeetUp.com, and www.JohnKerry.com.

In addition, you can join a special interest group working to defeat Bush such as the League of Conservation Voters, A.C.O.R.N., or Planned Parenthood. Please visit the chapter on "Democratic Activism" to learn more about special interest groups.

If you do wish to join an existing group, please, still READ and USE this chapter. Much of this information still applies to existing groups and should especially be helpful to an individual who has never participated in an organized political group before.

Starting Your Own Group:

If you are interested in forming your own group, first contact nearby groups (NOW, Sierra Club, NAACP, Democrats, etc.) preparing to take action against Bush in '04. Determine if they have compatible actions and goals as you. If so, work with them. They're already organized and overlapping actions will be less effective. If not, by all means form your own group and tell the nearby groups members about your group, ask them to participate, and to spread the message.

Organizing with others can be the most memorable part of a political activist's experience. It offers the opportunity to converse with like-minded people, share ideas, develop friendships, and of course, come together for the common purpose of defeating George W. Bush in 2004.

Before you start your own group, make sure you have the time, energy and skills to run a group successfully. If so, your first task is to find three to five others who are equally committed to your idea and will share the burden of leadership. Being the only one in charge is no picnic.

Next, agree on your goal and the actions you'll take to achieve it. Whether the goal is improving media coverage through protests or influencing Bush donors through boycotts. Have some ideas in mind so that you have direction.

Find People to Join:

After contacting local organizations, the long, hard process of finding members begins. Think of it in terms of marketing. You are trying to find citizens who want your product 'Helping defeat Bush in 2004', 'Improving the economy and health care', 'Our President to tell the Truth' along with many other possibilities. Consider where they might work, shop, and relax; what they read, listen to, and watch. These will give you clues as to where you're most likely to find like-minded individuals in your community. People equals power, plain and simple, so place great emphasis on recruiting. Consider contacting the following groups in your recruitment efforts: your local unions, environmental, women rights, minority, animal rights, places of worship, family, friends, relatives, co-workers, students, neighbors, community leaders, and whoever else you can think of.

Additionally, place an announcement in your local paper, put flyers up in public places, utilize the Internet and the local phone book, and if you feel comfortable, make your case in person. Get as many people as possible and always be on the outlook for new members. I highly recommend the websites http://www.Meetup.com and http://groups.yahoo.com for finding others who think like you.

Don't be discouraged if, at first, few people show up. The process of getting members is ongoing. The most important thing is maintaining the ones that you do get.

THE FIRST MEETING:

All of your neighborhood outreach is in anticipation for your first meeting, which is an extremely important first step. The first meeting is where you'll make your first impression and offer concrete plans for the group. When doing so, emphasize that your group will be pro-active. People join groups to do something meaningful and are often turned off by too many meetings.

Remember to be positive, cordial and respectful towards everyone's ideas. A welcoming atmosphere will make people feel comfortable. Outline tasks people can do before the next meeting. Additionally, remember:

- Don't let the meeting run too long.
- Stress the importance of making a commitment. Members dropping in and out not only is unhealthy for the group, it will make the effectiveness of your actions that much more unpredictable.

- Set a regular meeting day, time, and place for meetings.
- Ask how many are almost certain they will continue participating with the group now that they know more. Note this number so you know how many to expect at the next meeting.
- Give yourself a pat on the back if you get this far. Organizing a group is no walk in the park.

Between the first and second meeting, continue to promote the group and reach out for new members. The number of people who return for the second meeting will give you a clearer picture of how the first meeting went.

If most people come back, stay the course. If not, keep your head up and ask yourself and fellow members what changes can be made to improve membership retention.

THE SECOND MEETING:

Begin by thanking everyone who did show up for staying committed. At Your second meeting, a number of issues should be addressed: How will the group make decisions? Voting, straw polls, consensus? Who will shoulder responsibility? Delegating work will take a huge load off the core members.

You may need a secretary to keep minutes, a treasurer for donations and fundraising, someone to teach members about Bush's record, and a press secretary to work with the public and media.

Discuss the expectations and responsibilities of each position so Volunteers know what to expect. If people are reluctant, emphasize that the group's success is dependent on others taking leadership roles. Suggest people work together in an effort to lighten the work load and enjoy the work experience.

Planning Your Actions:

Then begin discussing and planning the actions you'll take. Planning actions should be a joyous relief since you're finally focusing on the reason the group was created in the first place. Planning will likely take more than one meeting and the logistics may constantly be changing, but remember, things don't have to be perfect before you take action.

You should already have an idea as to what method of action you desire to take, now is your chance to find others with a similar interest. Discuss with your fellow group members the various types of actions people want to take. If some members aspire to take an action that others don't, then by all means feel free to divide the group up into subgroups. Each subgroup can take their own actions, and perhaps as one large group you can take an action. This may be necessary because there are so many different actions to take and finding a consensus among many people is often times difficult. If you're unable to find anyone who desires to take the type of action you want, then consider doing it independently of the group.

Whatever path you decide to take, you must remain committed. This goes for everyone else in the group as well. You all depend on each other now, so if someone cannot commit, then they should take some other form of action. Keep in mind the time frame of the election as well. The election is Tuesday, Nov. 2. Have your action(s) be workable with the limited time available.

TAKING ACTION

Once your group has met a few times and is completely organized and prepared, the next step is taking action.

Plan with Goal

Decide how you will go about taking the action. Include a time frame, budget, strategy, necessary resources, and all other pertinent materials. The plan should also include a goal regarding what you hope to accomplish from your action. Examples would be to register 1,000 voters, go to 10,000 doors asking to vote Democrat, 10 positive Kerry articles in the paper, or handout 50,000 pamphlets. Whatever your plan make certain to have a reasonable goal or two in mind.

Perform

Eventually, it will be time to carry out the plan and take action. As you perform, assess how you conduct the action. Analyze what you're doing correctly or well and what needs improvement or is not working. Don't worry or panic if unforeseen problems arise. Be flexible to make adjustments to improve your plan. If your action involves the public, be conscious of your image. Always project yourself as courteous, friendly, and approachable. Being overly aggressive, arrogant, and rude will only turn potential voters off. Lastly, be confident in yourself and take pride in what you're doing. You are participating in your government, in a presidential election nonetheless; this should give you a plethora of stories to share with your kids and grand kids.

Review

Once the action is completed, review everything that occurred starting with how you organized and ending with what you've accomplished. Make changes to improve it for the next time. Organizing and taking action are not perfect processes, you can always look to adjust, change, and enhance.

Important Reminders:

Keep the following in mind when you begin to organize:

Communication

Decide how members will communicate. E-mail and phone trees are the most common. Decide on a time (if pertinent), and for what reasons you will contact each other. Also address how you will communicate during meetings in order to keep them from lasting eight hours. Raising hands and not interrupting people are highly recommended.

Becoming a Leader:

To make your group an enormous success, you and your core group will need to become outstanding leaders. The process will be gradual, but with practice and confidence your skills will grow.

As you lead the group, keep in mind that you're not perfect and don't know everything. Take criticism well, you can learn from it. Delegate work and acknowledge people when they've done their job well. Instill confidence in group members' ability to lead and perform well. Create a positive atmosphere, and try to instill in your group members a sense of unity, purpose, accomplishment, and being pro-active. If you are going to have any other leaders you must decide; media spokesman, secretary, treasurer, head of communications, head of education, and public relations are but a few possibilities.

And remember, while your work is serious and extremely important, it doesn't mean you can't enjoy it. Organizing will be a big part of successful action in 2004, so let's make it a worthwhile experience. Spice up your meetings with some food, music, a short video, or other enjoyable outlet

Decisions

Consider how the group will make decisions. Popular vote and consensus are common ways. Prior to deciding anything, make certain all voices that want to be heard are heard. Remember, everyone in your group has the right to vote, even people from Florida.

Money

Any action taken will most likely require the use of some money. Although it shouldn't be a large sum, the group must decide whether or not to conduct any fundraising or whether you will simply pool the necessary money and resources from members of the group. Some individuals may not have the money to spend while others may have a lot. Make sure you work the money situation out to everyone's satisfaction. In addition, when spending money at businesses; seek out those that are most friendly towards your efforts. Inquire if they will give you a discount. It never hurts to ask.

Education

It is crucial for the success of your actions that all members are educated on the issues of the campaign, the record of Bush, and the method of action you're taking. As a group, you must decide if people will educate themselves or whether to hold special education meetings. I can't think of many things worse than a reporter asking a question of a member of your group and having that member reveal they don't know what they're talking about. Moreover, if your action requires training, then do the necessary training. Being correctly prepared is vital.

Talents

Go through your group and ask what special skills each person has. Whether its computer skills, accounting, law, writing, activism experience, artistic talent, educating, security, detective work, research, fundraising, or whatever else you can think of. Find people's talents and utilize them to benefit your group's actions. In addition, find if anyone has a car, computer, copy machine, fax machine or other device the group may need to use.

Resources:

- For more help in organizing a group, go to
www.ActionForChange.org/getstarted.

Internet Activism Books: "CyberActivism" editors Martha McCaughey,
                                       Michael Ayers, and Michael D. Ayers
                                       "Electronic Democracy" by Graeme Browning.

Organizing Books: "Organizing: A Guide for Grassroots Leaders",
                              by Si Kahn
                              "Organizing: A Manual for Activist's in the 1990's" by
                              Kim Bobo, Jackie Kendall, and Steve Max.

4

The Bush Campaign

One of the most effective ways to stop Bush in 2004 could be through direct or indirect action that affects his campaign. My definition of a direct action is any effort where you directly confront the issue with your physical self. (Protest, civil disobedience, and sit-ins) Indirect actions confront issues but not in person. (Letters, handing out literature, phone calls) The purpose of taking action against the Bush campaign is to affect his money, time, message, and resources. The more money we drain from them, the less they have to promote Bush. The more time they spend dealing with us, the less time they have working for Bush. The more resources they use on us, the less they can use to benefit Bush. The more we get our message out, the less effective their message will be. All four; money, time, resources, and message affect Bush's ability to get votes. As a result; less votes for Bush and more votes for the Democrat, exactly the way we like it.

Taking action against the Bush Campaign is not for everybody. However, these methods could be very significant in harming Bush's chances of winning. Thus, they must be brought to the table so people have the choice. Before you decide on whether or not you're interested in this method of action, allow me to provide some words of caution.

Whether we like it or not, George W. Bush is considered the President of the United States. Security during the campaign will be second to none. The police and secret service will take no chances and will arrest you, whether legal or not, for almost any disruption. By no means should you antagonize law enforcement or be violent and give them a reason to arrest you. Always remain friendly, confident, honest, respectful, and work to get their vote. Though they may be overly zealous in arresting people, it is not your place to make a scene of it. Remember your image to the public; they are the ones we are trying to reach. Never forget that. Nonetheless, prepare yourself to be threatened, arrested, and physically harmed. This goes not only for the secret service, but the Bush supporters as well. I should know; I've lived through it.

During the 2000 campaign I protested Bush, by myself, for not allowing fair debates. While the overall experience was enjoyable, many moments worried me. Here are the ones I can remember: The numerous Bush supporters who vocally abused and harassed me. The CNN cameraman who assaulted me for getting in his picture and the Bush supporters whom, when I asked if they'd back me up if I told the police about the incident, bluntly lied and said they didn't see anything. Finally, the crazed Bush supporter who threatened me physically and actually came after me but was thwarted by the secret service, who surrounded me and moved him away.

While you may consider these examples dramatic and perhaps extreme, they are quite real. I emphasize these types of events because they do happen, and in some cases even worse. Thus, you should also consider Team Bush's response regarding direct actions against their campaign.

- For any direct action you take, expect Bush supporters already there expecting you. Their primary objective is to drown out your voice, your signs, and your message. They want to frustrate you and make you want to give up. Remain strong and remember your goal.

- Beware of what they say about you to the media. If you attend a rally, do everything in your power to get your message across through interviews, camera shots, and prepared press releases. Give them your answers to America's problems, offer alternatives to Bush's proposals and to his record. Create your own image as mush as possible, don't let the Bush team lie and put out disinformation regarding your nature and purpose.

- Beware of their scare tactics; threatening you with lawsuits, fines, and jail time. Be well aware of how legal or illegal your activities are before you follow through with them. If they are illegal, know the consequences before hand and be prepared to take responsibility for them.

FOCUL POINTS OF ACTION

The Bush Elite

The purpose of this method is many fold; disrupting Bush's campaign, taking media attention away from Bush and placing it on you, and telling the public what Bush is not telling them. When Bush Jr., Bush Sr., Laura Bush, Barbra Bush, Dick Cheney, Lynne Cheney, or any other Bush Elite makes a stump speech, has a rally, conducts a fundraiser, or any other high profile event in your neighborhood, take action. Conduct a Protest or Civil disobedience.

PROTESTS: Whether you protest or conduct civil disobedience, get as many people as possible to participate. Develop slogans and signs with a distinct message. For example, when I protested Bush I used an approximately 3" by 4" neon yellow piece of cardboard and on one side in bold black letters were the words "Fair Debates" while on the other it said "More Than two Candidates." Do not simply focus on the fact that Bush is dangerous for the country. Address the issues of the campaign; economy, homeland security, foreign policy, Bush's lies, etc. Having more than one issue is good, but more than three and I think the media's attention span will wane. Brainstorm for the best word combinations that exemplify your group's purpose. Take your time on the message; it will represent your group to the public. Be prepared to talk to the media. Prep yourself on questions they will likely ask. Also, have literature prepared to hand out to the public. While most will likely be hostile towards you, some may be undecided voters who could be influenced by what you have to say. If you need a permit, obtain one prior to the event from the cities government. For the best possible results, be persistent. The more the public sees of you the more likely they will hear what you have to say and be interested. Repetition is extremely effective.

CIVIL DISOBEDIENCE: If you conduct civil disobedience, definitely have a large number of people or it will not be effective. Learn how to be disobedient through training, practice, and books. Certain methods are better than others for certain situations. Examine the setting you will be civil disobedient in and determine which method is best. Of course, if you conduct civil disobedience be prepared to be arrested. Whether you sit-in on the stage where the speech is to be given, the street where their car is to drive, or in another strategic place, understand they will not be kind towards you. I suggest having a member of your team in the audience with a camera to document the entire action. Do not conduct a civil disobedience that will be counterproductive. This would include blocking a public place such as a highway, railway, etc. This could result in the public becoming frustrated, angry, and completely missing the message. Remember, you're always working to get the public on your side. The actions you take should encompass this belief. A schedule of Bush's campaign stops should be available at his website www.GeorgewBush.com. Guaranteed; you will encounter resistance with this method.

Further Resources: "The Civil Disobedience Handbook", Editor James Tracy.
Websites www.Protest.net, www.Ruckus.org, and www.WarResisters.org.

Bush Campaign offices

Located throughout every state will be Bush Campaign offices. By simply contacting your local Republican party or the Bush website, you can obtain the exact whereabouts. These offices are responsible for getting votes, donations, and spreading the Bush message in your area. Consider protesting the campaign office and handing out literature in front of the office with facts about Bush's real record as President. Before taking the action, contact the media. Make it an issue that the Bush campaign is misleading the public about Bush's record, distorting Kerry's record, and not telling the truth about the real state of America.

The Convention

Due to the vital role the convention plays during an election year, especially so this year, it is extremely important to pay attention to it. The convention is the greatest free advertising time for political parties. No wonder that once the party's over, the candidate's approval goes up. The Republicans are well aware of this and have already developed a strategy to greatly boost Bush's approval. The Republican convention will be held in New York City from Aug.30–Sept.2, right before the anniversary of the September 11th attacks. If we do not address the convention, it is bound to give Bush a double bounce of approval, first from the convention, next from the anniversary of Sept. 11th. There is one great flaw of holding the convention in NYC which we must utilize; NYC is full of Democrats! It is our responsibility to do everything in our power to paint the picture of reality. It is our responsibility to drag the media attention away from Bush. It is our responsibility to tell the other side of 9/11. For example: How on Aug. 6, 2001 Bush was informed by the CIA that American planes may be hijacked by Al Qaeda, and Bush did nothing. (Washington Post, May 16, 2002, Dan Eggen and Bill Miller) If it is in your power to be in New York during early September, then please come and attend the massive protests that will be taking place outside the convention. All who attend the convention should expect the tightest of security, but it doesn't mean we have to fear, back off, or tone down our message. The convention is the perfect time for all those who are against Bush to gather in one common area, with one common message; Bush had his chance and failed miserably, it is time for a change.

If you're unable to attend you can still help in other ways. Send whatever money, resources, and ideas you can to organizations protesting. Contact media outlets and tell them to cover the protests, not Bush's infomercial. Moreover, while the convention is taking place conduct a protest in your own neighborhood outside a Bush Campaign office. Get the media there so that all the news in your local media is not purely Bush, but also the people who were protesting him outside his offices. There will be hundreds of Bush campaign offices. A coordinated effort to protest NYC and the offices during the convention could get much attention and drown out some of Bush's propaganda. Visit www.CounterConvention.org and www.RNCNotWelcome.org

Education and Awareness

While the Presidential campaigns overall image, message, and perception are important, the deciding factor of the campaign may be the thousands of volunteers reaching out for support in their local areas. You can work on educating people regarding the negative side of electing Bush or the positive side of electing the Democrat. As you educate, consider having a petition to sign for the people you meet. The petition could address a campaign issue, an aspect of Bush's record, or a current bill being debated in congress. Here are some tips on educating people.

APPEAL TO PEOPLE'S SELF-INTEREST: Whenever you're trying to educate or persuade someone, appeal to their self-interest. People want to know what's in it for them, so tell them. Ask what issue they care about most and tell them how the candidates stand. Know why the Democrat is better than Bush and be able to express it in words. Have enough knowledge in your head to effectively address the weak and strong points of both Bush and the Democratic stances.

CREATE HANDOUTS: In order to educate people you'll need to create educational materials. Well organized and produced pamphlets, brochures, posters, and leaflets work well. If you focus on why Bush is bad, address his record, the campaign issues, and what four more years could mean for the country. Use facts and bring up many subjects to cover the various types of audiences you will be encountering. Keep them simple, mild mannered, and straightforward. As always, keep in mind your public image.

WHERE: Hand them out at local festivals, sporting events, malls, mall parking lots, college parking lots, subway entrances, concert venues, train stations, local tourist attractions, public gathering spaces, theme parks, and movie theatres just to name a few.

The Bush Team

In the first edition of this book I suggested citizens could hire a private investigator, investigative journalist, or lawyer to look into possible illegal activities by members of the Bush team which would disrupt their campaign. To my amazement it has come true. Not from a citizen investigating team Bush, but from team Bush forcing an investigation on themselves. Because "two senior administration officials" leaked the name of a covert CIA agent, there has been an ongoing investigation to discover who leaked the name and committed a felony. As the investigation continues, so does the pressure it puts on the Bush campaign. This distracts from Bush's message and forces those working for him to focus their time and energy on concerns which don't deal with Bush's "re"-election. Since the Bush team has proved there are some bad apples in the bunch, it is practical to think there may be more bad apples we haven't discovered yet. Below is a list of individuals working on the Bush Campaign. While it is unlikely they are all bad apples, there probably are a few. If you have the ability or the funds to weed them out, by all means do so. Though the public won't be able to see the trouble it causes in the campaign, you can be rest assured that behind closed doors the Republicans will be having a more difficult time. Also, take this time to educate yourself and become more familiar with who works for Bush.

- *Marc Racicot*—Chair of the Bush Campaign: Former Gov. of Montana who is known for his ability to raise soft money and helping Bush during the Florida recount disaster.
- *Karl Rove*—Advisor to the President: Long-time Bush Advisor who many see as the brains behind the entire operation. His reputation is to play very dirty politics.
- *Ken Mehlmen*—Campaign Manager: Worked on Bush Sr. '92 Campaign. Has worked under Karl Rove and been director of Dubya's Whitehouse political affairs office.

- *Mercer Reynolds*—Finance Chairman for Campaign: Owned the oil company that bailed out Bush in '84. Was appointed ambassador to Switzerland for his financial contributions to Bush's 2000 Campaign.
- *Jack Oliver*—Deputy to Mr. Reynolds: Finance director of Bush's 2000 Campaign. Worked for many Republicans in the past including John Ashcroft and Kit Bond.
- *David Hearndon*—Campaign Treasurer: Lawyer from Texas who also worked on the 2000 Campaign.
- *Andrew Card*—President's Chief of Staff: Former lobbyist for the car industry. Was Secretary of Transportation under Bush Sr.
- *Karen Hughes*—Advisor to the President: Worked as Bush's communications director in the 2000 Campaign and was a senior advisor to Bush as Governor of Texas. Just one of the women Bush uses to soften his image.
- *Scott McClellan*—Whitehouse Press Secretary: Spokesman for Bush as Governor.
- *Grover Norquist*—Conservative Activist Leader: The most influential conservative activist and President of Americans for Tax Reform.
- *Jeb Bush*—President's brother and Governor of Florida
- *Ann Wagner*—Republican National Committee (RNC) Co-Chairman
- *Jim Dyke*—RNC headquarters Communications Director
- *Mario Rodriquez*—Chairman for the Pacific States
- *Molly Bordonaro*—Chairperson for the Northwest
- *John Sanchez*—Chairman for the Southwest
- *Vin Weber*—Chairman for the Plains.
- *Ralph Reed*—Chairman for the Southeast
- *Jo Ann Davidson*—Chairperson for the Ohio Valley
- *Warren Erdman*—Chairman for the Central Region
- *Warren Tompkins*—Chairman for the Atlantic Region
- *Leslie Gromis*—Chairperson for the Mid-Atlantic
- *Jim Tobin*—Chairman for New England
- *Bob Kjellander*—Chairman for the Great Lakes

Information regarding the Bush campaign can be found at his campaign website: www.GeorgeWBush.com or the Republican National Committee website www.RNC.org.

You can contact his campaign headquarters at:

Mailing Address:

Bush/Cheney '04, Inc.
P.O. Box 10648
Arlington, VA 22210

Phone: 703-647-2700
Fax: 703-647-2993
E-Mail: BushCheney04@GeorgeWBush.com

In Addition: you can contact the Whitehouse with your thoughts on the President:

Mailing Address:
President George W. Bush
The White House
1600 Pennsylvania Ave. NW
Washington, D.C. 20500

Phone Numbers:
Fax: 202-456-2461
Comments: 202-456-1111
Swithboard: 202-456-1414
Hearing Impaired Phone Number:
Comments: 202-456-6213

E-Mail
President@Whitehouse.gov
Vice.President@Whitehouse.gov

Anti-Bush Websites include:

www.StopBushin2004.com
www.ToppleBush.com
www.LegitGov.org

www.ResidentBush.com
www.WhiteHouse.org

www.Bushwatch.net,
www.UnansweredQuestions.org
www.Votetoimpeach.org
www.OneTermPresident.org
www.JustOneTerm.com

www.ReDefeatBush.com
www.StopGWBush2004.com
www.BushDraft.com
www.Dubyaspeak.com

5

The Democratic Campaign

While by no means perfect, the Democratic presidential candidate is the only viable candidate with a chance at defeating Bush in 2004. As I have already said, there is much room for improvement within the party and by no means am I advocating blindly supporting them. While you may disagree with the candidate on certain issues, they will be far less harmful for the country then Bush and his administration have been. They may actually do some good for the country. (Even more so if we continue to participate when the election is over!)

If you decide to volunteer for the Democratic Presidential candidate, even if it's just part time, never give up your own principals. No political party or presidential candidate will ever completely agree with you, but it is your job to find the party that has a chance at winning and agrees with you on most issues. Work within the party to keep the principles you agree with and to change those you are against. By working for your local Democratic presidential campaign you have the opportunity to do just that. In addition, you will most likely have much less organizing to do. The Democrats should already be well organized and craving for volunteers. Prior to contacting the Democrats, know what type of volunteer work you will and won't do. While there may be other volunteer opportunities available, here are some common jobs you could possibly do while volunteering for the democrats.

Register Voters—A Critical Action!

Reaching out and registering individuals who are undecided or not inspired to vote will, in theory, increase the votes the Democrat receives. The more people the Democrats register as Democrats, the greater their chance at defeating Bush. Before you start registering voters, you, the Democratic office, or the special interest group will need to contact the local government regarding the rules of registering voters. Each state is different. You may have to be trained and approved, certain locations may be off limits, and they may require registering before a certain date.

Registering voters consists of going door to door or setting up a table at a popular public place or local event. You will be talking to citizens about whether they are registered, would like to change their registration, and why it is so important to vote (and do more!) If you can, stress the importance of voting and removing Bush from office. Registering voters will not only help dethrone Bush, but more voters can result in more Democrats winning elections in other offices as well. (Governors, Congressmen and women, and Senators) Contact your local city hall and your secretary of state for more information.

Last 72 Hours

The last 72 hours up to election are the most important for a campaign. This is the time when you become a Foot Soldier for the Democrats. Foot soldiers go around their neighborhood and knock on people's doors. When the door opens, you introduce yourself as a neighbor, and ask if they would please vote for the Democratic Candidate. (If a child answers the door, ask for the adult). You are not looking to get into any discussions or arguments, simply ask politely, give them a piece of literature, and leave. This technique works very well due to its simplicity, the personal connection people create from living in the same neighborhood, and through talking face to face. When it comes down to three—four days before the election, every individual seeking Bush's removal should take this type of action. Moreover, this is the time when thousands of phone calls are made to remind people to vote and ask one last time for their support. The last 72 hours before the election are the most critical. If you feel so inclined, join the local Democratic campaign and do whatever work is needed. Take off the weekend, and if you're able, Monday and Tuesday.

Canvassing—A Critical Action!

This action is similar to being a foot soldier. The difference is that you won't stay in your own neighborhood and it is conducted throughout the entire campaign. A group of volunteers will drive to a pre-determined neighborhood with maps, campaign literature, and a rap. The rap is what you say to a person when they answer the door, essentially a greeting and some information. You ask for the persons support, give them some literature, and maybe talk to them a little about the candidate. The campaign will give you information on what to say and how to say it, so don't fret over not being trained, you will be. After a day of canvassing you really get the hang of it and look forward to traveling to new places, meeting with voters, and spreading the "Vote Dem" message.

As with the last 72 hours, this method of campaigning works extremely well due to its personal nature. Voters enjoy talking directly with a supporter and will be affected by your kind, courteous, and confident nature. The Republicans will use this action abundantly in the campaign, making it all the more important that we have people canvassing as well. We can't let voters hear but one side of the story, so please consider canvassing as your volunteer action.

Donate Money/Fundraising—Another Critical Action!

Money, as you may well know, is a huge factor in this campaign. President Bush will raise over $250 million for his "re"-election bid. It is essential that we provide the Democrats with as much money as we can afford. The more money they have, the more they can spread their message and increase their chances of winning. We must all donate to the campaign, no matter how little the amount may be. The maximum donation for an individual is $2,000. If you don't have that amount, please donate what you can. Each donation of $500, $100, and $50 add up to help us win. Take the time now to donate money to the campaign, and ask others to donate as well. This chance only comes around every four years, so let's not hold back.

Due to the Bush camps seemingly unlimited supply of rich individuals and corporations willing to donate money, the Democrats must get every dollar they can no matter how small it might be. If you yourself can donate to the campaign, then by all means do so. Otherwise, if you volunteer, look for ways they can cut back costs to save money and help them with raising funds. You will likely make phone calls, go door to door, or work on mailings. While it may be grunt work, raising money is essential for victory.

Education and Awareness

Take note of the "Education and Awareness" section in the Bush Campaign chapter and utilize it to benefit the Democratic Candidate. Reach out especially to minorities, women, young people, and the elderly. Educate voters on the Democratic candidate using literature geared as much as possible toward the group you're addressing. In addition, whenever you're reaching out to other voters, be on the lookout for more volunteers. If you get a positive response during an encounter, go a step further and ask if they'd like to volunteer.

Endorsements

Seek local political, business, union, and social leaders to endorse the Democratic Candidate. Have the endorsement publicized in the local media and consider publicizing the endorsement in local educational literature. People are influenced by endorsements, especially if it's someone they admire, envy, or respect. Think about timing when you try to publicize an endorsement. Well timed endorsements have an even greater impact. Example: Have a local business leader endorse Kerry when another poor jobs report is released.

Office Work

Not the most enjoyable of volunteer jobs but crucial in order to succeed. Office work consists of taking people's phone calls and e-mails, typing up necessary documents, making phone calls to remind and encourage people to vote for the Democrat, conducting research, co-coordinating with other organizations, and stuffing envelopes.

Convention

The Democratic convention will be held in Boston, Massachusetts from July 26th–29th. If you're in the neighborhood, go to the convention in support of the candidate. You will likely not be able to get inside, but you may have the chance to join others who will show their support from the outside with rallies and marches. This will be effective if many people participate and you obtain media attention. The public will not only see the candidate, but that thousands of Americans are rallying to support him/her. While the convention serves as a platform to advertise to the American people, it can also serve to inspire you, the citizen, and motivate you for the last months in the campaign, which happen to be the most important months. If you cannot attend the convention, support your local media's coverage. Request as much coverage as possible but always keep an eye out for any bias they may be taking against the convention or the candidate. Call them on it and don't get off the phone until they let you talk with a producer, editor, or major reporter.

Personal Advertisements

Place a sign in your yard, wear a button, put a bumper sticker on your car, a sign in your car window, a sign out your house window, wear a t-shirt, hat, patch, or whatever other form of advertisement you can think of. You are giving people a reminder and producing an alternative to thousands upon thousands of personal advertisements people will see of Bush. Numerous websites are dedicated to getting the pro-Dem and anti-Bush message out. Spend a few dollars at one of these websites, and if you can, purchase more to give away.

www.JohnKerry.com
www.SeeYaGeorge.com
www.ButtonShack.com
www.ToppleBush.com
www.DemocracyMeansYou.com
www.Democrats.com
www.ReDefeatBush.com
www.GWBush.com

Talents

Read the "Talents" section in the Organizing chapter and utilize them to benefit the Democrats. If the Democrats need certain talents and you know people who have them, do your best to get them to volunteer.

Spread the Word

Spreading the message consists of informing the public, your family, relatives, friends, co-workers, and acquaintances about voting for Kerry. This can be done through casual discussions, by giving them a pamphlet, magazine, or book to read, informing them of a liberal website, or wearing the message. The more people in this country who start to think, the more people we'll have to vote Kerry.

Letter Writing

The Howard Dean Campaign brought my attention to writing letters to independent and undecided voters. The Democratic Campaign can provide you with a list of names and addresses of those who are registered as independent voters.

They will provide all the materials you need (stamps, paper, envelopes, etc.) and then it is up to you to write a letter asking them to support the Democrat. Explain from your heart why Bush Jr. doesn't deserve four more years and why the Democrat is truly better. This action is great due to its simplicity, personal nature, and the fact that you can do it at almost any time and location.

GOTV and Vote!—A Critical Action!

GOTV, or get out the vote, is vitally important. On Election Day, thousands of volunteers will work to get voters to the polls, make certain people have voted, and encourage those who haven't voted to do so. This is the one-day everyone should take off from work and be a volunteer for the Democrats. Many political pundits think this election will come down to turnout and getting out the political parties base. Thus, we must work our tails off getting Democratic voters to the polls on Election Day. Make sure you've contacted the Democrats to work on Nov. 2.

As for voting, I know it's the most basic and obvious of actions, but I had to mention it. If you aren't going to be in your home state come election day; vote using an absentee ballot from your local government.

Special Interest Organizations

The Democrats have hundreds of special interest organizations supporting their efforts and will likely work to get them elected during the campaign. Special interest groups will emphasize a specific campaign issue, registering voters, raising money, canvassing, and educating voters. Here is a brief description of some of the most important special interest groups working to defeat Bush.

Special Interest Groups

www.MoveOn.org The largest online activist organization which works to represent the concerns of average Americans. By utilizing their 1.7 million plus members, they are able to give citizens a voice in the political sphere. They are adamantly in favor of a new President. They will raise money for ads and tell their members about actions to take during the Campaign. If you sign up for one special interest group, sign up for this one.

www.AmericaComingTogether.com Formed specifically for the 2004 Presidential Campaign, ACT will work incessantly on defeating President Bush by focusing on the all important swing states. They will register voters, canvass neighborhoods, educate voters, and help elect progressive candidates to office.

www.BushRecall.org Another organization formed solely to defeat President Bush. BushRecall will compile contributions from all over America to run anti-Bush ads in all important swing states. One individual can donate up to $5,000.

www.GoodGovernment.org Another organization dedicated to influencing swing states. Canvassing, registering voters, and getting to people to the polls on Election Day are there main areas of focus. Additionally, they will focus on educating citizens on a broad number of issues including civil liberties, Medicare, Social Security, and more.

www.AmericaVotes.org A vital new organization which is a coalition of over 20 non-profit groups. Together they seek to educate, register, and increase voter participation. I highly suggest visiting this website and getting involved with a special interest group that appeals to you. Just some of the groups and their issues are:

www.ACORN.org (Low-Moderate Income People)
www.AFLCIO.org (Labor)
www.LCV.org, www.Environment2004.org, www.SierraClub.org (Environment)
www.PPAction.org, www.NARAL.org, (Pro-Choice)
www.NAACPNVF.org (Civil Rights)
www.VoicesForWorkingFamilies.org, www.AmericanFamilyVoices.org (Working Families)

If you do work for a Special Interest Group, keep in mind that many are not allowed by law to publicly state their support or lack their of for a candidate. They must remain non-partisan. However, if voters have any common sense, they'll get the idea of who you support or don't when you educate them as to how Bush is harming workers, the environment, civil rights, choice, the poor, etc. Also, check out the Democrats website www.Democrats.org/Links and work through one of the listed organizations.

For more information on volunteering during the campaign, use the "Democratic Contacts" at the end of the book.

Advice to Democratic Presidential Candidates.

Make the campaign a people's campaign. One of the great joys of supporting Nader in 2000 was his ability to reach out and connect with the people. Not simply disenchanted Democrats and Republicans, but especially to people who would not have voted otherwise. His rallies garnered between 10,000 and 20000 people. The Democrats could easily do this and on a much larger scale, say 50,000 people in attendance at a football or baseball stadium. You could raise a substantial amount of money this way, it will energize and motivate members to work hard, and you will reach more people. Utilize your base of support. Word of mouth along with media coverage will spread your message. Secondly, only accept money from socially responsible corporations and make it an issue of the campaign. Corporate corruption and abuses are still in the public eye and on people's minds. Make a point that Bush accepts money from companies that hurt the environment, our health, our children, weakens our foreign policy, and remind them of his close relationship with Enron. Take the leap, go with the people, and leave irresponsible corporations behind. It's time to draw the line in the sand. Make irresponsible corporations a liability to the Republicans. Finally, and try not to laugh, but tell people the truth. Tell the truth about Bush's record, the consequences of his decisions, the four years that he has been a right-wing conservative. Inform the American public of the alternatives, of your vision, of the world that is possible if we change directions.

6

Media Activism

The media has perhaps the greatest influence on undecided voters. Perception of the candidates, the messages heard and discussed, and the questions asked or not asked are all greatly controlled and shaped by the mass corporate media. Their instruments are the T.V., radio, websites, newspapers, and magazines. They can use this great and powerful tool to the benefit or hindrance of candidates. They can be fair or biased, misrepresent the facts or be accurate, have balanced coverage or unbalanced, censor information or provide all relevant information. Since many American voters will form their opinion of the candidates based on the media's projection, it is essential for us who want Bush gone to influence the media in every way possible. The modern media is the most powerful modern tool for controlling how people feel, act, and think. What better way to influence how people vote then by using the instrument by which most people get their information and opinions? If you conduct media activism, start doing so today, continue through the election, and beyond whatever may happen after.

The objective of taking action against the media is to encourage fair, non-biased, honest campaign coverage. We cannot simply take action against an outlet because we want positive stories about the Democrat and negative stories about Bush. We must have a reason. We must find bias. This goes not only for how the media covers the campaign, but how they cover the advertisements from each campaign. It is their job to criticize the campaign ads when they are false or deceiving. Remember this when watching the ads and the media's coverage of them. This chapter will focus on how we as citizens can influence the media when we find bias and how to use other forms of media which people tend to forget. Before taking action, you must decide on an outlet to take action against.

THE MEDIA OUTLET

There are many forms of media: newspapers, T.V., radio, Websites, magazines, and advertisements. Before you can influence the media, you must discover which type of media you hope to influence. Perhaps your local town newspaper or your local television station. Or, maybe you want to aim higher and address a national television program or a major newspaper. Whichever outlet you choose, you will have to do a few things first.

RESEARCH: Research the media outlet you've chosen including; their staff (publisher, editors, news columnists) past articles on the candidates, their advertisers, and current articles on the candidates.

LOOK FOR BIAS: While conducting your research, look for bias in their coverage towards Bush, censoring, misrepresentations of facts, what questions they ask and don't ask, and what overall image they are projecting of the two candidates. Document the bias for your records. The organization Fairness and Accuracy in Reporting has excellent information on detecting bias in the news, check out www.FAIR.org for more information.

WHO TO ADDRESS: Once you've learned how to detect bias, decide if you are going to address the outlet as a whole, a certain reporter, or a particular program. The one you choose should depend on where you discover the bias. Before you take action, have a clear goal in mind. Examples are an article of apology, dismissal of the reporter, or evidence of fairer coverage. Now, you and your group can take the following actions.

METHODS OF ACTION:

Make Friends

According to the Pew Charitable Trusts Project for Excellence in Journalism, a study of 1,149 stories from 17 news sources during the 2000 Presidential Campaign brought to light the media's conservative bias. Stories considered positive: Bush: 24%, Gore 13%. Stories considered Neutral: Bush 27%, Gore 31%. Stories considered negative: Bush: 49%, Gore 56%. More positive stories for Bush, more negative stories for Gore. This is all the proof we need to justify becoming media activists for 2004.

One of the most effective methods we can use is becoming friends with the media. This doesn't mean you're going to call Tom Brokaw and tell him what he's doing right or wrong. Actually, influencing the gigantic media conglomerates is not on the top of our list. Our actions should first be focused on influencing the media we have the best chance at changing, our local media.

The first thing you'll want to do is pick a local newspaper, T.V. station or radio station and begin using their media on a daily basis. Being consistent is crucial. If you miss a day, then you're out of the loop. As already mentioned, visit the website **www.FAIR.org** to learn how to detect media bias, slants, disinformation, and all the other methods media use to push their hidden agendas.

Once you've practiced detecting bias and are confident in your abilities to do so, contact the media outlets editor, news editor, or producer and tell them about what you're doing. This person will likely be the person you always contact with your information about bias.

Let them know that you're a local resident and user of the outlet and that you have formed a citizens group to ensure the outlet covers the Presidential campaign fairly. Be courteous, non-threatening, and try to convince the outlet that what you're doing will benefit them and their users. Provide them your name, the group's name, and your contact information. Inform them you will contact them in the future should your group find bias.

From here on out, you will be a media watchdog. Whenever you detect bias or slanted reporting, you or someone from your group should contact the outlet.

Before you contact the outlet regarding the bias, be certain you're right. Double-check with two or more people just to be sure. You want the outlet to take you seriously so you must be correct. When you've decided you're correct, immediately contact the outlet. Don't ever wait until Friday to report bias found in Monday's program. Phone the contact you made previously and explain your position. Your main objective is to put pressure on them to report future coverage fairly. Ask them what they will do to ensure it doesn't happen again.

Once you've contacted them, document your conversation and the bias. Keep records for every time you contact, what was discussed, and the outcome agreed on.

If bias should continue, follow up with letters to the editor, op-ed pieces, and phone calls to more individuals. Keep the pressure at all times. Should the situation continue or get worse, other actions may be needed.

Letters

Write to the Editor of a newspaper, the producer of a radio or T.V. program, or a particular reporter or journalist. Depending on how their coverage is, tell them how you appreciate the fair coverage or how disappointed you are by their bias. Provide them with examples and explain why it is bias. Remember to be courteous, practical, and persistent. Include your name, address, and the name, date, and author of the story your letter is referring to. Always ask them to respond. Constantly writing letters during the campaign will let them know you are part of the audience they want to please.

Op-ed Pieces

An opinion editorial is an article of opinion written by you for submission to a newspaper or magazine. When you first read a beneficial story (helps the Democrat, hurts Bush) or harmful (hurts the Democrat, helps Bush) story, immediately write an opinionated response. Submit the article as soon as possible, make it between 600 and 1200 words, and use original arguments. If you get an op-ed or letter published, tell others, it will inspire them to do the same.

Phone Calls

If letters and op-ed pieces don't work, phone the outlet. Speak with journalists and reporters first. Tell them you don't appreciate biased news (provide examples) and request them to change their method of coverage. If you see no changes, move on to the bosses; the editors, producers, publishers, and CEO's. Tell them your views. Remind them it is their duty as reporters of the news to be fair, unbiased, balanced, and accurate. If there is still no change, you may want to consider direct forms of action.

Visit: www.NewsLink.org and www.MondoTimes.com to find media outlets.

A CAMPAIGN AGAINST THE MEDIA

Before you start

Remember, much more time, energy, money, and people are needed to campaign against an outlet, especially if it's a national news outlet. Carefully consider if you can devote the necessary energy to effectively run a campaign. If you go ahead with a campaign, continue to take action through letters, op-ed pieces, and phone calls. Keep the pressure on at all times in all areas. Beyond a doubt a campaign directed at a local outlet has the chance of being more successful then one towards a national outlet. However, if you feel so inclined, begin a large campaign against Fox News, The Wall Street Journal, The New York Post, or whatever large outlet you discover being biased.

Contact Advertisers/Boycott

Research the outlets major advertisers that would be easy for the public to Boycott. Notify the advertisers of your campaign and show them your documentation of the outlets bias. Ask them to please refrain or cut back their advertising at the outlet. Inform them that if they continue to support the outlet, then they are supporting biased news coverage, and your group will begin a boycott. If they continue advertising, your group must decide as to whether or not you will follow through with the boycott. Should you choose to boycott, conduct it at the same time you are protesting the outlet. If the company stops advertising, then you have a very important victory. Inform the media outlet that due to their biased coverage advertisers are leaving. Perhaps now you will have their attention.

Protest/Boycott

During your boycott of the media outlets advertisers, protest and boycott the outlet as well. While you're protesting, hand out educational material to citizens passing by. The literature you hand out should state very clearly why you're protesting with examples of the bias and what the average citizen can do to help in your campaign. A massive educational/awareness campaign will be needed if a boycott is to be successful. Protesting in front of the outlets place of business, corporate headquarters, or in heavily populated public spaces will most likely give you the best exposure. As always, get as many local groups and local celebrities to garner support. In addition, work to obtain media coverage from the competition regarding your protest and boycott. They may not feel inclined if they think they are your next target. Tell them they're not, make friends, and get them on your side. If the other media outlets begin covering your story make the most of it. Please read the "Protest" section in the Bush Campaign chapter for more information regarding protests.

Civil Disobedience and More

If you conduct Civil Disobedience, go to the offices of the outlet and conduct a sit-in. Conduct it at their desks, chairs, floor, elevators, hallways, and whatever else that will keep them from doing their job. Other possibilities include the parking lot, the entrance way, news vans, and helicopters. Work to get coverage of your event from other outlets. Other possible actions include refusing to allow reporters the opportunity to broadcast in public spaces. Whether the report is live or recorded or whether it is a story about the presidential campaign or not. Any time they attempt to broadcast a story, be there and be heard; make your voice of dissent heard during reports and interviews, place signs behind the reporter, block their views, and don't stop talking to them about their biased coverage. Keep their phone lines tied up so they can't do their jobs. Hit them where they least expect it. Make them wish they reported fairly. Make them so frustrated that they have only two options: they stop doing their job, or start doing their job correctly. Uncommon methods of action on a large scale could have profound, unforeseen effects. For more information on Civil Disobedience, read the "Civil Disobedience" section in the Bush Campaign chapter.

Further information: "Prime Time Activism" by Charlotte Ryan
                  "Making the News" by Jason Salzman and visit the
                  website
                  Websites: www.FAIR.org/Activism
                  www.ReclaimTheMedia.org.

THE OTHER MEDIA

There is more to the media during a Presidential election than the corporate news and campaign advertisements. The following is a list of other methods of action using additional aspects of the media.

Paid Advertising

Yes, you, the average citizen, can take an ad out against Bush or for the Democrat. Of course this has the potential of costing a lot of money. However, if you have the money, know someone who does, or want to pool your money together with others, then it is quite possible and in many cases very reasonable. Costs will vary depending on many factors. (Time, length, number of airings, etc.) If you are interested in taking out a paid ad, research where and how you can best reach the most people at the most cost-effective price. Also, know your strengths and weaknesses in advertising. Are you able to do this on your own or will you need help from a professional? Does one particular media outlet (newspaper, T.V., radio) appeal to you more than another? You can advertise in so many places it's overwhelming. Here are just a few ideas. National, Local, and Cable Television, Newspapers, radio, magazines, billboards, Internet, sides of buses, subway stations, newsletters, direct mail, large public events, and private events (concerts, sporting). For information on ads during the campaign, visit www.BushOut.TV

Free Advertising

Free ads are excellent cheap ways of reaching large numbers of people. In some instances free ads can reach more voters than paid ones. All you have to do is pay for the material resources (paper, ink, makers, cloth, etc.) Some ideas could be against the law, so be aware of the consequences and ready to take responsibility. Free advertising ideas are; signs over highways, along highways, over water towers, grocery stores, libraries, bookstores, posters, coffee shops, and college campuses.

Radio/T.V. Talk Shows

If you happen to be watching the T.V. or listening to the radio and they start taking callers to talk about the campaign, call them up. Tell them why you are voting Democrat and why Bush doesn't deserve another 4 years. If you are successful at getting on the air, share it with others so that you might inspire them to call as well. Please visit the website www.Radio-locator.com to find the stations near you.

Support Alternative News Sources

While the vast majority of America is stupefied by the corporate media message, there are many who everyday turn to other sources for their news. For other perspectives on the election, read, watch, and listen to alternative media sources. If you're looking for reasons why, here are three:

In February of 2003, Clear Channel, the owner of over 1200 radio stations, organized pro-war rallies encouraging President Bush to attack Iraq. In June of the same year, despite enormous public outcry, corporate media successfully convinced the Federal Communications Commission to allow further media consolidation. And one month later, conservative columnist Robert Novak leaked the identity of a covert CIA operative sighting "senior administration sources", a.k.a., a big wig in the Whitehouse. Though the leak was an act of treason and detrimental to America's 'war on terror', big media ignored the story until the CIA woke them up. (International Herald Tribune, Paul Krugman, 3/26/03, www.PBS.org, June 2, 2003 interview with FCC Chairman Michael Powell, USA Today, Peter Johnson, 10/1/03)

When war, self-interest, and the hard truth are at stake, corporate media proves time and again they cannot be objective. For these reasons and countless others, we must seek out additional sources of news for the Presidential Campaign.

Now you may be asking yourself "What does this have to do with defeating Bush?" I can't stress enough; this has everything to do with winning in 2004. The corporate media has practically given Bush a free ride since 9/11/01 and the result has been disastrous. 69% of Americans think Iraq had something to do with 9/11. 69%! 9/11/01 is the biggest story of our time and the corporate media blew it. (www.Boston.com, Anne E. Kornblut and Bryan Bender, 9/16/03)

We cannot stand by and simply hope their coverage improves for the presidential campaign.

Supporting independent media outlets is important for numerous reasons.

- They have different viewpoints which are usually more informative, useful, and correct.

- They are not corrupted by a constant need to increase profits or to please advertisers.

- Supporting independent media is a statement to the corporate media that you are not satisfied with their news coverage.

- Independent media knows the difference between entertainment and news, and the news they provide more directly affects the peoples lives.

- Independent media is usually run by the people and for the people, as the media should be.

After all of this, you'd probably like to know what defines an alternative outlet. Well, there is no set definition I'm aware of. However, alternatives usually have the following in common: They are not considered mainstream, they are not beholden to shareholders, and they have a left or right wing slant. If you don't yet use alternatives, now is the time to start.

For our purposes, the liberal Alternatives should have the most beneficial coverage of the Presidential Campaign. The following is a list to get you started but by no means the only alternatives available. Use this list to get yourself acquainted with alternatives. Check them out, find the ones you enjoy, and use them regularly.

Daily News Websites: CommonDreams.org, Truthout.org, Zmag.org, Alternet.org, Buzzflash.com, Counterpunch.org, Salon.com, and AntiWar.com

Alternative Radio Programs: Meria.net, Alternativeradio.org, NewDimensions.org, WebActive.com, DemocracyNow.org and look for local radio programs.

Magazines: The Nation (weekly), In These Times (Bi-weekly), The Progressive (monthly), The American Prospect (Monthly) and Mother Jones (Bi-Monthly). In addition, they have excellent websites full of information.

Writers: Some of my favorite author websites include: www.GregPalast.com, www.MichaelMoore.com, www.JimHightower.com, and www.SanderHicks.com.

T.V. News: When it comes to obtaining alternative news via the T.V., watch **Free Speech T.V**. and visit **www.FreeSpeech.org** to find out how to get it. Other wise, the next best thing is BBC America. Additionally, www.GNN.TV has wonderful programs.

Liberal Web logs: www.DailyKos.com, www.TalkingPointsMemo.com www.LeanLeft.com, and www.TheLeftCoaster.com.

Movies: *Bob Roberts, Roger and Me, Uncovered: The Whole Truth About the Iraq War, Platoon, Manufacturing Consent, Unprecedented: 2000 Presidential Elections, Life and Debt, The Day After, and All the Presidents Men.*

Liberal Radio Stations

An offshoot of Alternative media is supporting liberal radio programs. I know it may sound surprising for some to learn that liberal radio actually exists since all the mainstream media talks about is Rush, Savage, and Hannity. I am here to tell you it does exist and is thriving in local communities across America. While the liberals are currently working to create a national liberal talk radio show, we can support the liberal talk show hosts that already exist in or around our local towns. With many of the shows, not only can you listen via radio, you can listen for free online. Please take time to support liberal radio by listening, donating money, and telling others about it. Some liberal radio shows include:

www.LouieFreeShow.com (Cleveland)
www.GuyJamesShow.com (Naples)
www.MikeWebb.org (Seattle)
www.DougBasham.com (Las Vegas)
www.TheRandiRhodesShow.com (West Palm Beach)
www.DemocraticTalkRadio.com
www.RadioInsideScoop.com
www.MikeMalloy.com
www.AirAmericaRadio.com

For more liberal hosts visit www.DemocraticUnderground.com and www.Buzzflash.com.

Comedy Outlets

From the Daily Show to David Letterman, The Onion magazine to Tom Tomorrow comic strips, the comedy we will see during the election campaign should be hilarious, but more importantly, it will have influences on how people think about the candidates. Whether the effect is on a conscious or subconscious level, political comedy can shape our views. For this reason, it is essential to maintain an influence over what comedy is popular. Thus, take some time to enjoy yourself and watch the Daily Show, read The Onion, or whatever comedy outlet you enjoy. If they say something to make Bush look bad, thank them and encourage them to continue. If they say something to make the Democrat look bad, tell them you don't like it (even if it is funny) and to concentrate their efforts on poking fun at Bush.

Visit: www.TheDailyshow.com, www.ThisModernWorld.com www.CBS.com/lateshow, www.NBC.com/Tonightshow

Creativity

Use your own special creativity to influence the media in ways I haven't expressed. If you're good at film making, then consider creating a short film regarding a subject of the campaign. If you're an artist or musician, create a work with a political statement. If you enjoy ad busting, then adbust the Bush Campaign's message and advertisements. (Visit www.Adbusters.org for information on ad busting.) Share your creations with the public, get them media attention, and use them as educational tools. For all I know, you could have the ability to start your own website, Internet show, radio program, or local public access T.V. program. Whatever your talent is, put it to use if it makes you happy and will influence voter's minds. Two creative websites spreading the 'Stop Bush' message include: www.RunAgainstBush.org and www.VoteBushOut.Biz

7

Student Activism

Student activists are the heart and soul of America. They are everything Americans should be. Student activists are passionate, idealistic, informed, and involved. Every American should be as involved as student activists. College campuses are a vibrant place of dialogue and exchange between groups and individuals with different viewpoints. I love seeing individuals take action when they're young. Not only college students, but high school, Jr. High, and elementary school students as well. One of the actions I'm most proud of is teaching elementary and Jr. High school students to stand up for what they believe in and take action. Young people are an underestimated demographic which will one day break out of it's shell and do something spectacular.

While students are welcome to address any of the other methods of action in the book, there are additional actions which students alone are best qualified and prepared to take due to their unique situation. Millions of students in high schools and colleges across the country are itching to make a difference in the world. They have the time, energy, and optimism to address the issues they care about most. If you want something to do on Friday and Saturday night, how does working to stop the election of a president sound? While this section is geared toward college students, the actions can be slightly altered for high school, Jr. High, and elementary school students as well.

Background

I must start by saying we do have an uphill battle to climb. A CNN/Gallup poll conducted in 2003 showed 61% of college students approving of President Bush's job with the same number stating the war in Iraq was the right decision. Since 9/11/01, college students have been much more inclined to support President Bush and the Republican Party. According to the College Republicans

National Committee, their membership has tripled on college campuses in just three years.

By reaching out to youth during the 2004 election, not only can we halt this disturbing trend, we can reverse it. By focusing on youth oriented issues and getting more youth involved, we can bring the young Americans back to the Democratic Party. With 28 million people between the ages of 18–24, we would be fools to concede the youth vote to the Republicans.

I believe the first and primary objective should be education. By educating young voters on the issues that are most important to them, we can prove to them beyond any doubt that President Bush has failed and should not be elected. Here are the three issues to focus on:

JOBS: Jobs under President Bush have been particularly awful and youth should respond well to these facts. The number of college graduates hired out of college was cut 36% in 2002. 42% of employers reduced starting salaries for college graduates in 2003. George W. Bush will be the first President since Herbert Hoover to have a net loss of jobs during his administration. Bush will never be able to claim he's the 'job security' president. (www.CNNFN.com, Leslie Haggin Geary, 7/3/03, "Salary Cuts for Grads")

MILITARY STRENGTH: Due to 9/11/01, the strength of the military consistently remains one of the top issues students care about. Under President Bush, our military moral and re-enlistment has plummeted. Dubya gave us the impression that the war in Iraq would be easy and quick, and it has been neither. The Iraq war has increased terrorism in Iraq, taken the focus off Al-Qaeda, and increased Al-Qaeda's membership.

DRAFT: Related to military strength but a separate issue for students is the possibility of a military draft. Due to our stretched military and decreases in enrollment, President Bush is quietly creating the foundations for a draft. A recent posting on the U.S. Department of Defense website sought 'Selective Service System Local Board Member." When it started to garner media attention, the posting was conspicuously removed. If Bush is "re"-elected, the argument can be made that a draft is more likely. (www.BushDraft.com)

In addition to following the "Education and Awareness" section in the Bush Campaign chapter, also focus on making students aware of how significant it is to vote, especially in this day and age when our rights are being taken away from us.

Excellent locations to conduct education efforts include campus sporting, social, and academic events. You may want to attend a sporting event yourself and hold up a sign saying "Vote Democrat." There are an abundant amount of places and ways to make people aware.

While I have been stressing the education of youth on college campuses, don't overlook groups such as professors, the administration, maintenance, food staff, coaches, and numerous other positions. If you can, also get these people involved with your group. At the least, reach out for their vote and give them some literature. By showing you care about every vote, you have a chance to reach them. College campuses are excellent places for reaching large numbers of people.

Form a Group

Use the organization chapter to help you get started on building your own campus group. Whether the group will be officially recognized and receive funding, or be unofficial and broke, is for you to decide. If you become official, you should qualify for funding from your college. Requirements vary by college, but the most common include; a group name, purpose, who can join, a budget, a faculty sponsor, and how elections will occur. I started a student organization my senior year in college to address the issues of developing countries. Here are three tips of advice from what I learned while on the job.

APPROVAL OF THE GROUP: Talk with student council members, who will likely have to approve the organization, and whoever else may have to approve it and get them on your side. Work on this before you begin working to get the group recognized, you will just be wasting time if council members say there is no chance they'll approve of such a group.

DELEGATE WORK: Give members responsibilities to keep them active, involved, and recognizing they are needed. Emphasis the need for people to stand up and take leadership positions. Attempting to do everything yourself will leave you overworked and unenthused.

STRESS COMMITMENT: Stress the importance of every individual committing to the group. Many times students float in and out of a group. If you're to run successful actions against Bush, it is imperative that all know the importance of showing up to meetings, getting their work done, and taking part in the actions.

If forming a group is not your style, look into joining a group on campus that may already be involved in a campaign against Bush. Most obviously are the campus Democrats, Environmental clubs, Women's Rights, Black Rights, other minority groups on campus, Animal rights, Human rights, Workers rights and Developing countries. Find the groups taking action and work with them.

Coalitions

If you've formed your own group, reach out to other campus organizations which may be inclined to assist you in your efforts, such as the groups listed above. Contact the Presidents of the groups and ask them to inform their organizations members regarding the idea. If you do work together, seek common ground regarding what actions everyone is comfortable with taking. If the members decline, remind them they are all welcome to join your group as well.

Another consideration is coordinating with other colleges who are similarly taking action against Bush. Contact colleges in your area, go to their websites, and talk to students to determine if they have groups working against Bush. Your groups can work together on one action or coordinate actions you take. For example, students from all over the country walking out of class in protest of Bush's policies or election campaign. Or, students going to the local republican campaign office and protesting. Keep it dramatic and invite all media to write a story.

College Media

The college media can serve numerous purposes. First, use it to announce your group's first meeting and welcome any and all who are interested to join. If your school has campus wide e-mail, announce it this way as well. Second, make the formation of your group a news story. Ask the newspaper and radio to conduct a story on you, and, once again, ask for students to join. Throughout your campaign, make press releases to your college media outlets and your local community outlets regarding the actions you take. Invite them to write a story regarding *every* action you take.

Endorsements and participation

Work to obtain well-known and well-respected professors, athletes, and students to endorse the democratic candidate and participate in your efforts. Every school has famous athletes, professors, board of trustee members, and students who others look up to. They have the ability to influence students as well as faculty and other college employees. After obtaining their support, work to get the endorsement covered by, you guessed it, the media.

Alumni

The college alumni office is a great organization to work with early and get on your side. They have access to tens of thousands of graduates, or in many cases hundreds of thousands or graduates. Work to get something in the Alumni newsletter, which most colleges possess. Even if it's just a mention of your group, any little exposure you can obtain will help in the long run. Every little thing affects us and makes a difference. If you can think of other methods of utilizing the alumni, go for it.

Community Outreach

Don't limit yourself to just the college campus. Go out into your local community and register voters, educate people, and use an action method from one of the other chapters in this book. Moreover, reach out to the people of the community. Let them know you care about more than your college, that you are inclusive, and that they matter. Go door to door, local community events, or well populated sites. (Grocery store, mall, library, etc.) In order to be more effective within the community, and on campus for that matter, contact local organizations involved in the election. Ask them for advice, exchange ideas, and if you so desire, work together on taking a particular action.

HIGH SCHOOLS, JR. HIGHS, AND ELEMENTARY SCHOOLS

If you're a student in high school, Jr. High, or elementary school, this paragraph is for you. Please take action at your school in whatever way you enjoy or believe will have the greatest impact. Use the actions mentioned above and modify them for use in your own school. Let your teachers, principle, and fellow students know you will not sit quietly and allow the Bush administration to jeopardize your future. You have the strength and ability to determine your own opinions, ideas, and actions. Know your rights. You have the right to free speech. You have the right to speak out against the president. You have the right to speak out against war. You have the right to say who you support. Authority figures have been controlling you all your life. Break free, start educating yourself, and start taking action now. The sooner you begin, the better your future and that of the worlds will be.

Further reading: **"Take Action", by Craig Kielburger and Marc Kielburger**
"Teen Power Politics" by Sara Jane Boyers
"Generation React" by Danny Seo.

Websites: Student Environmental Action Coalition www.SEAC.org, College Democrats, www.CollegeDems.com, Young Democrats of America, www.YDA.org, www.StudentPeaceAction.org, www.CampusActivism.org, and www.WireTapMag.org.

8

Economic Activism

One of the most effective strategies to ensure Bush is not elected would be a mass movement of people cutting back the amount of money they spend or boycotting companies that donate to Republicans. First, let's focus on consumer spending.

The economy is the central focal point of American life and politics. If the economy is doing well, probability wise politicians are re-elected. If it is doing poor, they are voted out. Thus, the most common sense strategy to stop Bush is for the people who don't support him as president to curb their consumption, to reduce their spending. There are two good arguments to reduce your consumption.

Every dollar I spend helps keep Bush in office. The more I spend, the stronger the economy and an increased chance Bush will be elected. Thus, every dollar I reduce my consumption by hurts Bush's chance of being elected that much more. If the 50 million Americans who voted for Gore in 2000 reduce their monthly spending by 1%, there will be a slight effect on the economy. If they reduce by 5%, we will have people taking notice and getting nervous. If they reduce by 10 %, we will have the rest of the America calling for a regime change as well.

The second good argument to reduce consumption is with every dollar we spend, we make a political statement in support of the current U.S. administration; in support for the current political leadership. Since spending money is a political statement, by cutting back, we make a statement that the leadership must change their ways or step down before we start spending money again. Not spending money is a powerful political statement. By realizing how our money directly effects who is in office, we are taking the first step of taking responsibility for how we spend our money. We realize how our money affects the world and how we spend it says what we approve or don't approve of. Politics is just the tip of the iceberg. Later on we may start realizing how spending money on an SUV supports global warming and a reckless foreign policy, buying certain wood products supports destroying the rainforest, and buying certain clothes supports child labor. In most of these cases we do have a choice; we are not trapped by "the system."

Now, I realize some readers will say cutting back your spending to hurt the economy is bad for your community and could end up hurting you. You are potentially correct. That is why I give you these words of advice. Go as far as you feel comfortable, as far as your conscience will allow. You must way the costs and the benefits. Costs: possibly damage the economy of my local community and my own place of employment. Even this analysis may be flawed because having Bush and company in office could harm the economy and your place of employment even more so. (But not if you work for Exxon or Lockheed Martin) Benefits: Contribute to the possible de-throwing of Bush, reducing harm to the environment, not supporting corrupt corporations, realizing how my money affects the world, having more money to use as savings, pay down debt, or pay for children's education. The purpose of reducing consumption is for the *long-term* benefits of having a president who is concerned about the WHOLE of America, not just a PIECE of America. Bush's policies have great potential to hurt America long into the future, even more so if he's allowed another four years. The following is a list of various ways to take action.

DEVELOP A PLAN OF ACTION

Assess your monthly expenditures and your willingness to cut back. Everything you spend money on in a month; from rent, car payment, insurance, food, entertainment, transportation, vacations, pets, electricity and other bills, credit card and other debt should all be organized. Once you recognize what you spend your money on, find the ways you are comfortable in cutting back. Here are some suggestions:

Reduce Your Overall Consumption

You can reduce your consumption across the board by a certain amount, say 10%, or on certain items such as food, restaurants, clothing, movies, cds, event tickets (sports, concerts, musicals, etc.), magazines, phone/cable/Internet service, vacations, etc.

No Big Ticket Items

Commit yourself to not purchasing any large consumer items such as cars, refrigerators, computers, dishwashers, TVs, digital cameras, washer and dryer, housing improvements, stereo systems, furniture, etc. If you must by one, try to purchase it used with a warranty.

Minimize Transportation Cost and Use

Do your best not to spend money supporting the automotive and oil industry, major supporters of the Bush administration. Use public transportation, bike, walk, carpool, rollerblade, scooter, unicycle, horseback, fly, boat, swim, scuba dive, or parasail.

Stop Using Credit Cards

Rather than use your credit card, commit yourself to paying cash. Save your credit cards for an emergency. Moreover, your finances should be healthier because you won't be buying items you don't need with money you don't have.

Place of Work

Encourage co-workers to donate money to the Democratic campaign and to not donate to the Bush campaign. Moreover, if you have the ability to cut back on how much your company spends, do your best to cut back spending and investment. The more you cut back, the less the economy grows, the less likely Bush is elected.

Tell Other People

While it sounds simple, many people don't tell others they are cutting back the amount they spend. Perhaps people believe it is not their job to change other people or to offend them. But to be realistic, cutting back spending is not going to work well unless many people do it. By telling someone they are supporting Bush by spending money you are giving them a choice. Most will not have realized it. Now it is up to them to decide whether or not to continue the same as before, or to join the ranks of the responsible and cut back. Word of mouth is the most underestimated tool.

For Further information on economic activism visit the websites
www.NewDream.org and www.CorpWatch.org, www.ibuydifferent.org.

BOYCOTT BUSH DONORS

A plethora of corporations donate money to political parties and candidates thereby helping those candidates win election, and, making the candidate feel accountable to the needs of those companies. Regular employees, bosses, and the companies PAC provide the companies with an outlet to donate money to candidates. Both Republicans and Democrats accept money from them. However, many corporations donate much more to Republicans and President Bush than they do to Democrats. This is an obvious sign of support for President Bush and his 're'-election in November. While there are still many companies that donate to Democrats and favor Democrats, it would be impossible to boycott all corporations at once. The most logical and effective starting point is boycotting corporations who have already chosen sides in the political ring by donating more money to Bush and Republicans. While the long-term goal is to get corporate money out of politics all together, the short-term goal is to reduce the money corporations give to Bush and Republicans

It is counterproductive to purchase goods and services from companies that want President Bush elected. We are giving them more money to give to the President. The more we spend, the more they can give to Bush, increasing his chances of winning. With a large and sustained boycott, corporations will have less money to donate to Bush and the Republicans, less incentive to do so (since business will be hurting), and a greater incentive to stop all-together (since they'll want business to get back to normal).

You can affect the Presidential campaign by boycotting the companies listed below, sending a letter to the company telling them you will boycott, and rallying others to join in the cause. We can defeat President Bush in 2004, but it will take a lot more than wishful thinking. We must take action and affect the amount of money going into his campaign. Join the boycott to take back America from the special interests and return political power back where it belongs, with the American people.

For further information **visit www.FEC.gov (Federal Election Commission), www.OpenSecrets.org and www.PoliticalMoneyLine.com,**

Who to Boycott?

While I know it may not be possible to boycott all of the companies below, please do your best. This information was taken from the non-profit, non-partisan website www.OpenSecrets.org in late January of 2004. Many of the amounts will have changed, but the discrepancies in donations will likely remain the same, if not grow larger. The graph shows: Organization: The name of the company to boycott. Amount: How much money the company has given to both parties combined. Dem: The percentage of that money which has gone to the Democrats. Rep: The percentage of that money which has gone to Republicans. Visit www.BoycottBush.org for more information.

Financial Institutions:

Organization	Amount	Dem.	Rep.
Citigroup Inc	$891,505	42%	58%
Morgan Stanley	$753,182	41%	59%
Merrill Lynch	$713,725	16%	84%
PricewaterhouseCoopers	$586,554	15%	85%
Ernst & Young	$561,434	31%	68%
Credit Suisse First Boston	$555,750	37%	63%
Deloitte & Touche	$529,810	28%	72%
MBNA Corp	$519,225	16%	84%
KPMG LLP	$519,040	22%	78%
UBS Americas	$507,051	22%	77%
JP Morgan Chase & Co	$427,695	34%	66%
Bear Stearns	$427,083	29%	71%
Wachovia Corp	$390,066	13%	87%

Oil Companies:

Organization	Amount	Dem.	Rep.
Valero Energy (Shamrock)	$208,400	16%	84%
Exxon Mobil	$136,870	9%	91%
ChevronTexaco	$102,200	15%	85%
Marathon Oil	$87,358	13%	87%
BP (Amaco)	$78,700	38%	62%
ConocoPhillips	$52,998	25%	73%

Pharmaceuticals:

Organization	Amount	Dem.	Rep.
Pfizer Inc	$437,210	34%	66%
GlaxoSmithKline	$360,296	28%	72%
Eli Lilly & Co	$310,022	24%	76%
Johnson & Johnson	$305,300	38%	62%
Merck & Co	$251,205	28%	72%
Abbott Laboratories	$174,837	18%	82%
Schering-Plough Corp	$93,000	18%	82%
Bristol-Myers Squibb	$86,475	28%	71%
Aventis	$78,500	32%	68%
Bayer Corp	$70,050	24%	75%

Restaurants/Fast Food

Organization	Amount	Dem.	Rep.
Outback Steakhouse	$219,250	2%	98%
Darden (Red Lobster, Olive Garden)	$64,204	19%	81%
Wendy's	$52,550	20%	80%
McDonald's	$47,928	16%	84%
Waffle House Inc	$30,200	0%	100%
YUM! (Taco Bell, Pizza Hut, KFC)	$27,113	6%	94%
Burger King Corp	$26,000	3%	97%
Dunkin Donut Franchise	$25,300	0%	100%
Cracker Barrel Old Country Store	$23,000	9%	91%

Retail Sales:

Organization	Amount	Dem.	Rep.
Wal-Mart Stores	$1,049,850	15%	85%
Limited Brands	$129,250	17%	83%
Gap Inc	$115,000	47%	52%
Home Depot	$101,250	0%	100%
Circuit City Stores	$84,500	4%	96%
Sears, Roebuck & Co	$76,500	21%	78%
Target Corp	$64,950	26%	72%
JC Penney	$50,816	17%	81%
Walgreen Co	$50,400	33%	67%

Tech Companies:

Organization	Amount	Dem.	Rep.
Gateway Inc	$71,000	35%	64%
eBay Inc	$60,250	41%	59%
Dell Computer	$59,700	30%	69%
Texas Instruments	$51,400	18%	82%

Telephone

Organization	Amount	Dem.	Rep.
SBC Communications	$874,166	32%	67%
Verizon Communications	$427,461	33%	66%
BellSouth Corp	$339,860	41%	59%
Sprint Corp	$155,150	40%	60%
IDT Corp	$74,950	20%	80%

Tobacco

Organization	Amount	Dem.	Rep.
Altria (Phillip Morris, Kraft Foods)	$396,450	44%	55%
RJ Reynolds Tobacco	$274,200	14%	86%
UST (Skoal, Copenhagen)	$218,649	11%	89%
Brown & Williamson Tobacco	$76,450	16%	84%
Lorillard Tobacco	$27,500	15%	85%

Transportation

Organization	Amount	Dem.	Rep.
United Parcel Service	$897,030	28%	72%
FedEx Corp	$392,020	35%	65%
Ford Motor Co	$294,574	24%	76%
DaimlerChrysler	$250,590	39%	61%
Enterprise Rent-A-Car	$193,700	9%	91%
Delta Airlines	$105,239	28%	72%
Continental Airlines	$68,646	30%	70%
Southwest Airlines	$27,500	16%	84%
America West Airlines	$15,200	28%	72%
US Airways	$15,000	28%	66%

9

Bush's Record

The following is a very brief record of Bush's first three years in office. While there is much, much more to know, this information will give you a start on educating yourself regarding Bush's record as President and provide a clearer picture as to why we are taking action. The issues covered include; the economy, homeland security, social security, environment, energy, military personnel, civil liberties, and foreign policy. For more information please visit the website of the Democrats, www.Democrats.org/SpecialReports, The Center for Constitutional Rights, www.CCR-NY.org, In These Times www.InTheseTimes.com, and the websites listed in the 'Education' chapter.

Economy

- Under the Bush Administration, an estimated 2.7 million Americans have become unemployed, an increase of 43% from when Bush took office. As of February 2004, the national unemployment rate was 5.6%. Over 10% for African Americans. (Bureau of Labor Statistics 3/04)

- There has been a 186% increase in long-term unemployment (27 weeks or more) since Bush took office. As of October 2002, it stood at 1.9 million. (Bureau of Labor Statistics, 10/4/02).

- The Bush tax cut passed in 2001 gave 47.7% of the tax cut to those in the top1% of the tax bracket. 9.5% of the tax cut went to the bottom 80% of tax payers. (New York Times, 12/22/02)

- The CBO (Congressional Budget Office), a non-partisan governmental agency, has projected the 2004 budget deficit to reach 477 $Billion. (CBO January 2004)

- The 10 year deficit is projected to be $5.2 trillion; $7.6 trillion if you take out the $2.4 million in social security surpluses. (Center on Budget and Policy Priorities, 1/28/04)

- The IMF (International Monetary Fund), an international institution largely financed and controlled by the United States, issued a report in January stating "large U.S. fiscal deficits also pose significant risks for the rest of the world." In other words, we're threatening the global economy. (IMF, 1/7/04)

- In December of 2003, the economy produced only 1,000 new jobs, increasing the likelihood of a jobless 'recovery', if you can call it that. (Bureau of Labor Statistics, January 2004)

- In May, 2003, the President passed yet another tax cut, further increasing deficits and decreasing government income. According to Citizens for Tax Justices, in 2003 and 2004, 47% or more of Americans will get less then $100 with the average tax cut for these 65 million plus tax payers coming in at $19. In 2005, the average tax reduction for 97.9 million tax payers will be $5. (Citizens For Tax Justice, 5/30/03)

Homeland Security

- With President Bush's encouragement, Senate Republicans slashed $9.8 Billion from the omnibus FY2003 bill H.J.RES.2. A majority of the cut was felt by homeland security: border, port security, airports, mass transit, food safety, and state and local assistances grants. (New York Times 1/16/03, Wall Street Journal 1/16/03)

- President Bush's justice department decided to freeze all grants meant for first responders—fire fighters, emergency medical personnel, and police. The money was to be used for training and equipment by state and local governments. (Los Angeles Times, 12/3/02, Washington Post 12/4/02)

- In October of 2001, the Democratic Party proposed the creation of a Homeland Security Department. It took 239 days before President Bush decided to support the idea. (S.1534. Congressional Record pg. S10646 10/11/01, Presidents address to nation 6/6/02)

Social Security

- The Social Security Trust Fund will be drained from now until the year 2010, when Bush's first tax cut is set to expire. During these seven years, an estimated $1.5 Trillion in Social Security Funds will be used for other purposes. If the Bush administration gets their way and the tax cuts are made permanent, the raid on Social Security will continue. (CBO, Budget and Economic Outlook: An Update, Summary Table 1-1, 8/27/02; Bush Remarks to the Economic Club of Chicago, 1/7/03)

• The Presidents own Commission to Strengthen Social Security unveiled three different plans to help Social Security. Every single plan included a reduction in guaranteed benefits. The New York Times stated; "President Bush's Social Security Commission set out three options today for allowing workers to establish individual investment accounts and acknowledged that the proposals would have to be accompanied by benefit cuts or other painful steps if the retirement system was to overt a long-term financial crisis" (New York Times, 1/30/01).

• A USA Today Editorial states "The Refusal of the White House and Congress to tackle the looming crisis is bad enough. What's worse is that they are hastening Social Security's collapse by diverting billions of dollars needed to repair it to finance other programs and tax cuts. The Bush Administration now admits that the budget deficit this year will top $200 billion and that's after the government spends $171 billion in Social Security surpluses on programs other than retirement benefits." (Editorial, USA Today, 1/20/03)

Environment

• In Sept. 2002, the Bush Administration devalued every American life by $2.4 million. In a report released by the EPA regarding the benefits of regulating pollution from electric generators, snowmobiles, engines in forklifts, and all-terrain vehicles the EPA used a new form of analysis. The traditional analysis placed the benefits of regulation at $77 Billion, while the new method placed the benefits of regulation at only $8.8 Billion. The great discrepancy is due to the fact that traditional analysis valued a human life at $6.1 million, while Bush's EPA valued a life at $3.7 million, and only $2.3 million for citizens over 70 years old. (Washington Post, 12/10/02)

• Due to pressure from the coal and oil industry, President Bush reneged on his campaign promise to reduce carbon dioxide pollution, a major cause of Global Warming. (Bush Speech: A Comprehensive National Energy Policy, 9/29/00 Saginaw, MI AP, Washington Post 3/14/01, Bush letter to Senator Chuck Hagel, 3/13/01)

- In early 2002, the Bush Administration released a new interpretation of the Clean Water Act which would greatly cut back Federal Regulation in "non-navigable" waterways such as streams. As a result, an increase of dredging and filling and waste dumping can take place in these waterways. (Newsday, 1/12/03, Sierra Club Press Release, 1/6/03)

- The famous Montreal Protocol, signed by Ronald Reagan in 1987, meant to phase out the use of nearly all ozone-depleting chemicals around the world. President Bush, however, has fought the protocol and argued for increasing the use of Methyl Bromide, the most powerful ozone depleting pesticide. (NRDC, 11/14/03)

- President Bush proposed changes that would allow power plants to emit mercury 10 year longer than they would have been allowed to under President Clinton. The Clinton rules set the reduction deadline at 2008, while Bush has extended it to 2018. Mercury is a highly toxic and unhealthy chemical which can cause brain damage, especially in infants and children. (www.CommonDreams.org, 12/05/03)

Energy

- The Republican energy bill introduced last fall, which President Bush supported, would provide over $10 Billion in tax breaks to the oil and coal industry, $30 Billion in subsidies to nuclear energy, and fails to increase the use of renewable energy. After the blackout that stretched from NYC to Detroit last summer, one would hope the people would come before the campaign contributors, but it is obviously not the case with Bush. (Sierra Club, 2003)

- The United States currently imports 55% of its oil supply. By 2025, it is expected to increase to 68%. (Energy Information Administration "Annual Energy Outlook 2003 with Projections to 2025" 1/9/03).

- Bush has pushed drilling for oil in the Alaskan National Wildlife Refuge (ANWR). The Energy Information Administration stated it would take 10 years from the day of production before any oil was extracted, and 20 more years before full production would occur. They also projected a decrease in dependence of foreign oil from a projected 62% to only 60%. (CNN "Inside Politic," 4/10/02, Natural Resource Defense Council "Ending America's Oil Dependence," Jan/02)

- Renewable energy programs funding was slashed in President Bush's FY 2003 budget. The Congressional Research Service states "major cuts in proposed spending include decreases of $15.7 million for distributed Energy, $11.3 million for Concentrated Solar, 6.2 million for Biopower and 2.6 million for Program Direction." (Congressional Research Service, "Renewable Energy: Tax credit, Budget, and Electricity Production Issues" 2/6/02)

- Bush issued an increase in fuel standards for light trucks and SUV's by 1.5 mpg over the course of five years. All other cars fuel requirements stayed the same. The Natural Resource Defense Council writes: "According to the National Academy of Sciences, fleet-wide fuel economy could be raised by more than 10 times the amount proposed by the administration. Because passenger vehicles use about 40 percent of the 19 million barrels of oil consumed in the United States each day, the administration's proposal will perpetuate the nation's dangerous dependence on foreign oil." (Natural Resource Defense Council, Press Release 12/12/02)

Military Personnel

- As Commander in Chief, President Bush went to war with Iraq in the spring of 2003 where the military once again used weapons containing depleted uranium. "Uranium is a by product of enriched uranium, the fissile material in nuclear weapons." states the magazine In These Times. Moreover, they assert that "Dr. Rosalie Bertell, a Canadian epidemiologist, released a study in 1999 revealing that depleted uranium can stay in the lungs for up to two years. When the dust is breathed in, it passes through the walls of the lung and into the blood stream, circulating through the whole body...represents a serious risk of damaged immune systems and fatal cancers." The 1991 Gulf War resulted in a sickness now known as "Gulf War Syndrome" which the defense department has been unable to completely explain. An estimated 300,000 troops from the first Gulf War now suffer from various medical conditions ranging from "...excruciating muscle and joint pain, headaches, chronic fatigue, memory loss, and blackouts..." Depleted Uranium was also used in the first Gulf War. The Bush administration has done nothing to stop the use of Depleted Uranium. (In These Times, July 21 P.14, Weapons of Mass Deception, by Frida Berringan, You Back The Attack, We'll Bomb Who We Want, Remixed war propaganda by Micah Ian Wright and Commentary by The Center For Constitutional Rights, P. 92)

- Some Veterans were required to pay 45% of their health care costs each year, up to $1500, due to Bush's FY2003 budget. (The Independent Budget Press Release, 2/20/02)

- Bush's 2003 budget will also hit 160,000 veterans who will no longer be able to receive medical services. (Associated Press, 1/16/03, The Daily Oklahoman 1/18/03)

- Bush sought to increase the amount veterans pay for prescription drugs. Veterans making over $24,000 a year would have to pay a $250 to simply enroll and the co-pay would more than double from $7 to $15. Luckily, the Democrats beat this one. (Reuters, 7/14/03, Washington Post, 7/22/03)

- The Presidents 2004 budget cut $200 million from programs that help military kids obtain a decent education. (House Appropriations committee, 6/16/03, 6/17/03, Washington Post 6/17/03)

- The war in Iraq has created low morale and increased the possibility of many soldiers not re-enlisting. This could create a crisis in the U.S. military resulting in another draft. (Washington Post, 10/16/03, www. BushDraft.com)

Civil Liberties

- The Bush Administration has begun developing a program entitled Total Information Awareness, or TIA for short. The TIA project, while being sold to the public as a way to find "terrorists", has the potential to infringe upon every citizen's right to privacy. According to In These Times; "The TIA program proposes to process huge amounts of public and private data about U.S. Citizens and foreigners: bank transactions, cell phone and computer communications, casino transactions, gun purchases, car and video rentals, and medical transcripts are only some of the data sets the system is purportedly designed to scan and cross-reference." (In These Times: Big Liberty is Watching, July 21, 2003 Roberto Lovato, P.21)

- President Bush's Homeland Security department has begun reviewing the Posse Comitatus Act. This Act bans Military Personnel from conducting civilian law enforcement activities, which are usually left up to local and state police. If Posse Comitatus is overturned, the military could be used on its own citizens. (You Back the Attack, We'll Bomb Who We Want: Remixed War Propaganda by Micah Ian Wright with Commentary by the Center For Constitutional Rights, P.72)

- The Bush Administration passed the "Patriot Act" a new law sold to the public as a way to find terrorists, but has the potential to subjugate our fourth amendment rights to privacy. According to The Nation magazine, the law "allows the feds to explore the Internet, e-mail, computer hard-drives, and personal financial and medical records of people against whom there is insufficient or zero evidence, and allows their arrest without due process protections. Ashcroft conceded that he needed the new sweeping powers not to catch criminals in the act but to arrest anyone who seemed the slightest bit suspicious."(The Nation, posted October 30, 2001, by Robert Scheer, www.thenation.com/doc.mhtml?i=20011112&s=20011030)

- "Patriot Act II" is being drafted under the name "Domestic Security Enhancement Act of 2003." Some of the proposed "enhancements" include the authorization of secret arrests, expanding the crimes for which the death penalty can be used, allowing the government to wiretap citizens' homes without a court order, allowing the deportation of lawful U.S. residents, and creating a database of genetic information on American citizens without their approval or knowledge. (In These Times, 2/14/03, by Naureen Shah)

Foreign Policy

- Without United Nations approval, the majority of the international community opposed, unprovoked, and with millions of American citizens protesting, President Bush attacked and invaded the country of Iraq. Now, the United States is occupying another sovereign nation, controlling an oil supply that does not belong to them, and installing a government created by the United States and not the people of Iraq.

- In the process of leading the nation to war, President Bush along with many members of his administration may have lied or misled the American people in order to garner support. According to U.S. News and World Report "Veteran intelligence officers were dismayed. "The policy decisions weren't matching the reports we were reading every day," says an intelligence official. In September, 2002, U.S. News has learned, the Defense Intelligence Agency issued a classified assessment of Iraq's chemical weapons. It concluded: "There is no reliable information on whether Iraq is producing and stockpiling chemical weapons..." At about the same time, Rumsfeld told Congress that Saddam's "regime has amassed large, clandestine stockpiles of chemical weapons, including VX, sarin, cyclosarin and mustard gas." If they are proven to have knowingly lied or misled the country and congress, it would be a criminal act and the individuals responsible would be subject to impeachment and/or prosecution. (U.S. News and World Report, June 9, 2003, P.17)

- The President has already spent $166 Billion of American taxpayer money to fund the Iraq war ($79 Billion) and occupation effort ($87 Billion). (House.Gov)

- David Kay, former chief weapons inspector in Iraq, stated in January of 2004 that the Bush administration was "almost all wrong" when they said Iraq had weapons of mass destruction. This is extremely disturbing since Donald Rumsfeld, Dick Cheney, Condoleezza Rice, and George W. Bush repeatedly stated in the lead up to the war that there was "no doubt" Iraq had weapons of Mass Destruction. (USA Today, 1/28/04)

- As of March 5, 2004, 551 American soldiers have died in Iraq, 3,132 soldiers have been wounded, and approximately 10,000 Iraqi civilians have been killed. (www.AntiWar.com)

- Bush is pushing for the Defense Department to create so called "mini-nukes." As a result, he is increasing the chance that nuclear weapons would be used in standard warfare not only by the U.S., but other countries as well. This has the potential of starting a new arms race. In addition, it is hypocritical to publicly admit building *new* weapons of mass destruction while at the same time initiating war(s) with countries simply because they *might* have them. (You Back the Attack, We'll Bomb Who We Want: Remixed War Propaganda by Micah Ian Wright with Commentary by the Center For Constitutional Rights, P.86)

- Without consulting the Senate, which ratified the Anti-Ballistic Missile Treaty intended to "Curb the Proliferation of Nuclear Weapons", President Bush withdrew from the treaty in late 2001. The President, by withdrawing from this particular treaty, insists that he has the authority to terminate any treaty, and can do so without the consent of Congress. Through his action the President is setting a dangerous precedent, saying that any President can withdraw from any treaty they don't like and not consult the other branches of government which were required to pass it. Article I, Section I of the constitution of the United States provides congress with the power of creating laws and the President with the power to only implement the laws, not to repel them. In addition, Article 6, Clause 2 states that treaties are the "supreme law of the land." (You Back the Attack, We'll Bomb Who We Want: Remixed War Propaganda by Micah Ian Wright with Commentary by the Center For Constitutional Rights, P.86)

10

Parting Thoughts

While I am concerned as much as the next person at the possibility of having four more years of George W. Bush running the show, we must realize and address the issue that President Bush and his administration are but a symptom of a much larger problem in America. If we do not face the larger problems within our country, we are bound to have more Presidents like Bush in the future.

As long as corporations are able to funnel money to candidates, our Democracy will be vulnerable and our legislation will serve the moneyed interests, not the people. As long as the media is controlled by profit seeking corporations, our citizens will receive reporting that puts money and profits ahead of what is best for the American people. As long as citizens refuse to exercise their right to vote, participate, and influence the political world, our Democracy will be threatened. We are all responsible; the corporations, the politicians, the media, and the everyday citizen for allowing things to get this unbalanced.

Thus, whether we win or lose in November, we must not lose sight of the long-term goal. We must not lose sight of the big changes that are needed if real change is to occur. By participating in the 2004 Campaign to defeat President Bush, we are taking the first step towards those changes.

Win or lose, we must continue to demand a transformation in Washington. We must demand real Campaign finance reform, protection of Civil Liberties, reducing the power of the President, reducing corporate greed and power, getting rid of big media monopolies, creating a media for the people, making it easier for citizens to participate, along with numerous other changes.

The big changes I speak of are needed not only on the national level, but on the state and local levels as well. Our state and local political systems are in just as much need of these major changes. We must all get involved with our local, state, and national political scenes if any of the big changes we hope to see are to occur. Not only is the work meaningful and important, it is essential if we are to take control of our lives and destinies. For far too long have we allowed corporations, the corporate media, and the corporate controlled politicians tell us what is best for us. We must stand up and tell them what is best for us, and if they don't listen, lend our support to those who will.

The 2004 Presidential Campaign has great potential to put us on the track necessary for the big changes to occur. More and more people are participating in political discussions, reading alternative forms of media, waking up to corporate dominance over our lives, waking up to the military industrial complex, and realizing the need to get involved. With millions and millions of Americans turning on to politics, we can transform our country; one town at a time, one state at a time, one senator at a time, one law at a time, one President at a time; until we finally have the America we dream of.

Campaign Calendar

The following is a list of important events and dates to keep in mind for the 2004 campaign. Not all dates are set in stone or for that matter even announced yet. Please double check all dates prior to taking action.

January–March

- Democratic Presidential primaries held throughout U.S.

- Democratic Presidential candidate will be chosen by March.

April–June

- Extensive fundraising conducted by Democrats and Republicans

- Announcement of the Democratic Presidential candidate's running mate.

- Canvassing and Registering voters begins, especially in swing states.

July

- Democratic Presidential Convention in Boston, Massachusetts, July 26–29.

August

- Olympics held in Athens, Greece August 13–29. The media will pay much less attention to the campaign during this time.

September

- Republican Convention held in New York City, New York. Aug.30–Sept.2

- Third Anniversary of September 11th.

- Time to begin final two month push for Democrat.

- Daily political rallies as candidates travel throughout the U.S.

October

- Presidential debates held. (Visit www.debates.org for more information.)
- Weekend of October 29–31 begins last 72 hour push for Democratic Candidate.

November

- November 2, 2004 is the day of the election. Be sure to vote and remind others to do the same. If you can, take the day off and participate in GOTV efforts. Hopefully we will have a new president elect by the end of the night. No matter what happens, continue to stay informed and involved. Our future depends on it.

Democratic/Liberal Contacts

John Kerry Campaign

John Kerry for President, Inc.
519 C Street, NE
Washington, DC 20002
202-548-6800
202-548-6801 (fax)
www.JohnKerry.com

Donate **NOW** at 1-866-455-3779

Or, send a check, made payable to: John Kerry for President, Inc.
P.O. Box 77247
Washington, DC 20003

General Comments/Questions:
info@johnkerry.com

Webmaster:
webmaster@johnkerry.com

MeetUp Questions:
meetup@johnkerry.com

Kerry Campaign State Offices (If your state is not listed here, they did not yet have an office at the time of publication, please visit www.JohnKerry.com to find it.)

California Office—LA
6100 Wilshire Blvd.
Suite 225
Los Angeles, CA 90048

323-935-7034
323-935-2979 (finance)
323-935-3579 (fax)

California Office—SF
166 South Park #3
San Francisco, CA 94107
415-355-1470

Connecticut Office
99 Pratt Street, Suite 420
Hartford, CT 06143
860-524-0260

Florida Office
201 S. Biscayne Blvd
Suite 2700, Miami Center
Miami, FL 33131
305-372-9945
305-371-5732 (fax)

Georgia Office
1100 Spring St.
Suite 700
Atlanta, GA 30309
404-745-9189
Georgia@johnkerry.com

Idaho Office
877 Main Street
Suite 610
Boise, Idaho 83702

Illinois Office
432 N Clark St
Suite 203
Chicago, IL 60610

312-832-0220
312-832-0921 (fax)

Massachusetts Office
197 Portland Street, 3rd Floor
Boston, MA 02114
617-367-1551
617-523-2033 (fax)

Maryland Office
191 Main Street
3rd Floor
Annapolis, MD 21401
(410) 984-9046

Minnesota Office
8100 Wayzata Boulevard
St. Louis Park, MN 55426
763-540-0259
763-545-0018 (fax)

New Jersey Office
50 Northfield Ave.
West Orange, NJ 07052
973-325-2309
973-325-1999 (fax)

New York Office
373 Park Avenue South
9th floor
New York, NY 10016-8805
212-213-0220
212-213-9230 (fax)

Ohio Office
1480 Dublin Road
Columbus, OH 43215

614-340-1997
614-487-1051 (fax)

Pennsylvania Office
622 2nd Avenue
Second Floor
Pittsburgh, PA 15219
412-402-0351
412-562-2119 (fax)

Rhode Island
249 Roosevelt Avenue
Suite 202
Pawtucket, RI 02860

Texas Office
3200 Travis St.
3rd Floor
Houston, TX 77006
713-526-2004
713-526-3094 (fax)

Democratic National Committee

Mailing Address:
430 S. Capitol St. SE
Washington, DC 20003

Main Phone Number: 202-863-8000
Website: www.Democrats.org

Young Democrats of America

Mailing Address:
PO Box 77496
Washington, DC 20013-8496

Phone: (202) 639-8585
Toll Free: (877) 639-8585
Fax: (202) 318-3221
E-Mail: office@yda.org

Website: www.YDA.org

College Dems

Phone Number: 202-863-8151

Address
430 South Capitol Street, SE
Washington, DC 20003
Website: www.CollegeDems.com

House Democrats:

http://www.DemocraticAction.org—Help Democrats running for Congress.
http://Democraticleader.house.gov
http://Democrats.house.gov

Senate Democrats:

http://DSCC.org—Help Senators running for Congress.
http://Democrats.Senate.gov

Democratic Websites

www.DemocracyForAmerica.com
www.WellStone.org
www.Democrats.com
www.Democrats.us
www.DemocraticUnderground.com
www.DemsOnline.net
www.DemocratsAbroad.org
www.NDOL.org

www.ProgressiveMajority.org
www.ProgressivePortal.org

References and Further Reading

The Best Democracy Money Can Buy By Greg Palast
The Perfect Tie By James W. Ceaser and Andrew Busch
Bushwacked By Molly Ivans and Lou Dubose
The Bush Hater's Handbook By Jack Huberman
The Great Unraveling By Paul Krugman

The Lies of George W. Bush By David Corn
You Back the Attack, We'll Bomb Who We Want! with commentary by the Center
    for Constitutional Rights and remixed war propaganda by Micah Ian
    Wright.
Politics for Dummies By Ann DeLaney
Enough is Enough: The Hellraisers Guide to Community Activism By Diane
    MacEachern
CyberActivism Editors Martha McCaughey, Michael Ayers, and Michael D. Ayers

Organizing: A Guide for Grassroots Leaders By Si Kahn
Organizing: A Manual for Activist's in the 1990's By Kim Bobo, Jackie Kendall,
    and Steve Max.
The Civil Disobedience Handbook Editor James Tracey
Prime Time Activism By Charollote Ryan
Making the News By Jason Saltzman

Take Action By Craig Kielburger and Marc Kielburger
Teen Power Politics By Sara Jane Boyers
Generation React By Danny Seo
Politics and the Common Man By H.T. Reynolds
Take It Personally Editor Anita Rodick

The Activist's Handbook By Randy Shaw
Rules For Radicals By Saul D. Alinsky

Going Local: Creating Self-Reliant Communities in a Global Age by Michael J.
    Shuman
Non-Violent Resistance by Muhatma K. Gandhi

Current State of American Government

Power Trip: U.S. Unilateralism and Global Strategy After September 11 Editor
    John Feffer
*Silencing Political Dissent: How Post-September 11 Anti-Terrorism Measures
    Threaten Our Civil Liberties* by Nancy Chang
Secret Trials and Executions: Military Tribunals and the Threat to Democracy by
    Barbara Olshansky
Full Spectrum Dominance: U.S. Power In Iraq and Beyond by Rahul Mahajan
Against War with Iraq: An Anti-war Primer by Jennie Green, Barbra Olshansky,
    Michael Ratner
9-11 by Noam Chomsky
Terrorism and War by Howard Zinn

Additional Reading

1984 and *Animal Farm* By George Orwell
Brave New World By Aldous Huxley
The Autobiography of Malcolm X As Told to Alex Haley
Culture Jam By Kalle Lasn
Ishmael By Daniel Quinn

Non-Zero By Robert Wright
For the New Intellectual By Ayn Rand
The Continuum Concept By Jean Liedloff
One Flew Over the Cuckoos Nest By Ken Kesey
Cat's Cradle By Kurt Vonnegut

Reading Lists

George W. Bush

Bush's War For Re-election, By James Moore
The Price of Loyalty, By Ron Suskind

Worse Than Watergate, By John W. Dean
American Dynasty, By Kevin Phillips
Dreaming War, By Gore Vidal

Fortunate Son, By J.H. Hatfield
Against All Enemies, By Richard Clarke
House of Bush, House of Saud, By Craig Unger
Fraud, By Paul Waldman
Thieves in High Places, By Jim Hightower

Weapons of Mass Deception, By Sheldon Rampton and John Stauber
The Book on Bush by Eric Alterman
Had Enough? By James Carville
Dude, Where's My Country? By Michael Moore
Bush's Brain: How Karl Rove Made George W. Bush Presidential" by James Moore

Republicans

Blinded By the Right By David Brock
Big Lies, By Joe Conason
Lies and the Lying Liars Who Tell Them, Al Franken
The I Hate Republicans Reader, By Clint Willis
Perfectly Legal, By David Cay Johnston

The Corporate Media

Our Media, Not Theirs, By Robert McChesney, John Nichols
Rich Media, Poor Democracy, By Robert McChesney
What Liberal Media? By Eric Alterman
Media Control, By Noam Chomsky
Inventing Reality, By Michael Parenti

Politics and American Government

The Declaration of Independence and The Constitution of the United States
The Irony of Democracy By Thomas R. Dye
Democracy For the Few By Michael Parenti
A People's History of the United States of America By Howard Zinn

Democracy In America By Alexis De Tocqueville
Common Sense By Thomas Paine

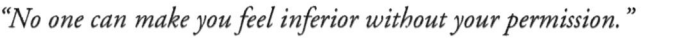

"No one can make you feel inferior without your permission."

—Eleanor Roosevelt

0-595-31644-1